Before th

MW01120430

Navigating the Turbulent Road of College Football Recruiting

By: Jeffrey C. Mitchell
and Taylor J. Mitchell

This book was written to assist high school student-athletes and their families in navigating the recruiting process. Each individual's experience will be different, because there is no exact formula or science as to how it works or what will happen. What we do hope that this book can serve as a guide for your family and answer some of the questions that you may have. There is no golden ticket to receive a full-ride scholarship anywhere in this book. But there are years of insights gained from our family's experiences with our four college recruits, as well as the insights of others that we've spoken with over the years. We want you to understand all of the opportunities that exist and how to reach them. Educating yourself on the recruiting process is the first step in discovering what opportunities may be out there for you. Good luck in your search!

About the Author & Contributors

Jeff Mitchell has been married to his wife Rhonda for 25 years and together they have raised their five children. Their lives have been dedicated to staying engaged in their kids' lives and to serving their community. Jeff has been an active volunteer for over 20 years working with children and youth in various roles:

- Little League Baseball coach (14 years)
- Youth soccer coach (17 years) with a National "E" Level License
- Select baseball Coach (9 years)
- Youth basketball, floor hockey, and YMCA pre-school sports coach (12 different teams)
- Youth director for a church youth group (4 years)
- Director for a large church pre-school midweek program (4 years)
- High School Booster Club Volunteer
  - Basketball club webmaster (2 years)
  - Football Booster Club (6 years), serving 1 year as Vice President and 5 years as President.

The Mitchell's children, sons Taylor, Josh, Nick & Caleb and the youngest, daughter Sara Kaitlyn, have all been active in athletics since their earliest days playing soccer, baseball, basketball, floor hockey, snow skiing, track & field, cross country and wrestling. All four boys have played or are playing college football.

Taylor played Division II Football at Humboldt State University in California. He was a team captain and starter at inside linebacker in his senior season. Taylor played in all 44 games of his 4 year career, which concluded with the school's first trip to the postseason in 48 years and their first post-season victory in 50 years. Taylor was recruited by DII, DIII, NAIA and DI-FCS schools (as a preferred walk-on). He is currently an Assistant Recruiting Specialist for the University of Washington Football program. Previously he served as the Recruiting Coordinator and Linebackers Coach at Humboldt State University.

Josh played Division I Football at Oregon State University. He was a team captain his senior year and a two year starter at Center. He played in 48 consecutive games, including 10 his freshman year, starting in a total of 27 games. He was voted to the First Team AP Pac-12 All-Conference Team at Center in 2015. Josh is the Offensive Line Coach and Run Game Coordinator for his high school alma mater, Mount Si. He is also serving as the Head Wrestling Coach for Mount Si.

Nick played Division I Football at Oregon State University. He was a quarterback, redshirting in his first season and competing with six other quarterbacks for the starting job in 2015. He eventually started 5 games before choosing to transfer to Cerritos College in January 2016. Nick currently plays for Southern Oregon University, a NAIA school.

Caleb plays Division I- FCS Football at the University of Montana. He is a long-snapper who also played safety on the scout team as a redshirt in 2016. In high school he was a 3 year letterman at defensive back, wide receiver and long-snapper. He was actively recruited by DII schools before accepting a preferred walk-on offer at Montana.

Each of the Mitchell sons had a different path as they pursued the opportunity of playing college football. Their experiences were unique due in part to the different positions that they played, their varying abilities, and different physical attributes.

As Football Booster Club President, Jeff had the opportunity to be involved in the lives of numerous high school student-athletes and their families as they also navigated the road to playing college football. This book is Jeff's attempt to share the insights and lessons that his family learned through the experiences of his own sons and as well as many other players. Taylor adds insights from his perspective as a brother who helped guide his sibling through the recruiting process, as a player, and college football coach.

The process of finding the right college FIT for your son is one that can draw you closer as a family and help your son to mature as a young adult. May you enjoy the ride!

TABLE OF CONTENTS

GLOSSARY

Recruiting Terms

Commit – (noun) A player that has given a "verbal commitment" (see below) (A verbal commit officially becomes committed when they have signed their NLI or Financial Aid Agreement, this is the difference between a commit and a verbal commitment). (verb) When a player gives a verbal commitment to a school.

Contact – A contact occurs any time a college coach says more than hello during a face-to-face contact with a college-bound student-athlete or his or her parents off the college's campus.

Contact Period - During a contact period a college coach may have face-to-face contact with college-bound student-athletes or their parents, watch student-athletes compete and visit their high schools, and write or telephone student-athletes or their parents.

Dead Period – During a dead period a college coach may not have face-to-face contact with college-bound student-athletes or their parents, and may not watch student-athletes compete or visit their high schools. Coaches may write and telephone student-athletes or their parents during a dead period.

Early Signing Period - Still a proposal for the NCAA to pass, it has not been enacted. The proposal would make accommodations for a 72-hour early signing period beginning in mid-December, the same time as the Junior College signing period.

Evaluation Period - During an evaluation period a college coach may watch college-bound student-athletes compete, visit their high schools, and write or telephone student-athletes or their parents. However, a college coach may not have face-to-face contact with college-bound student-athletes or their parents off the college's campus during an evaluation period.

FBS – Football Bowl Subdivision, also referred to as Division I-A or DI. The highest classification of NCAA football. Teams make the post-season to play in Bowl Games. The 4 top teams play in a single elimination championship tournament, but begin by playing in Bowl Games.

FCS – Football Championship Subdivision, also called DI-FCS, formerly referred to as Division I-AA. The second highest classification of NCAA football with teams competing in a single elimination tournament at the end of the season that concludes with a championship game.

Grayshirt - Takes place when a player postpones their arrival to a college campus typically because of roster and scholarship limitations, will usually arrive to campus after the fall and will join the team and will then begin receiving their scholarship. A student-athlete essentially sits out for a semester, is not enrolled in school, on the football team or receiving any financial aid. A grayshirt typically takes place in the fall because of roster/scholarship limitations which may not allow for an incoming freshman to be on the team until the spring.

National Letter of Intent (NLI) - A National Letter of Intent is signed by a college-bound student-athlete when the student-athlete agrees to attend a Division I or II college or university. Participating institutions agree to provide financial aid for one academic year to the student-athlete as long as the student-athlete is admitted to the school and is eligible for financial aid under NCAA rules.

NAIA - National Association of Intercollegiate Athletics, comprised of more than 250 Colleges and Universities and 21 Conferences.

NCAA - National Collegiate Athletic Association comprised of 1,121 Colleges and Universities, 99 voting Athletic Conferences, and 39 affiliated organizations. (6)

Offer (scholarship) - An offer is a non-binding offer made by a college coach to attend their school. This offer can be a scholarship offer, but it can be pulled/revoked by a coach at any time. There is nothing binding until an NLI is sent by the school and signed by the student-athlete.

Official Visit - Any visit to a college campus by a college-bound student-athlete or his or her parents paid for by the college is an official visit. During an official visit the college can pay for transportation to and from the college for the prospect, lodging and three meals per day for both the prospect and the parent or guardian, as well as reasonable entertainment expenses including three tickets to a home sports event.

Preferred Walk-on - Is a guaranteed spot on a team/roster that does not include any financial aid. Preferred Walk-on's can't sign a National Letter of Intent so this agreement is non-binding, but there is a possibility for a scholarship in the future. Schools may send out an agreement for Preferred Walk-on's to sign, but there is nothing binding and this student-athlete may choose to not attend this school.

Quiet Period - During a quiet period, a college coach may only have face-to-face contact with college-bound student-athletes or their parents on the college's campus. A coach may not watch student-athletes compete (unless a competition occurs on the college's campus) or visit their high schools. Coaches may write or telephone college-bound student-athletes or their parents during this time.

Redshirt - What a "redshirt" season refers to is a year in which a student-athlete does not compete at all against outside competition. During a year in which the student-athlete does not compete, a student can practice with his or her team and receive financial aid.

Unofficial Visit - Visits paid for by college-bound student-athletes or their parents are unofficial visits. The only expenses a college-bound student-athlete may receive from a college during an unofficial visit are three tickets to a home sports event.

Verbal Commitment - Just like an offer, this is a non-binding statement made by a prospective student-athlete to accept a school's offer to play for their team. At any time, the school can pull this offer and a student-athlete can decommit from this particular school.

Walk-on - This occurs when a student-athlete tries out for a team. They can be competing with others for a roster spot and initially will not be on a football scholarship. Based on roster limitations, some schools will not allow for walk-ons to come out while other schools will have tryouts when school starts or once the season is over.

7 Day Signing Period – If a National Letter of Intent is not signed by a student-athlete and their parent/legal guardian and I do not sign this NLI and accompanying offer of athletics aid within 7 days after the date of issuance (noted on the signing page) it will be invalid.

College Athletics

Achievable Goal or Fantasy?

1

I remember the moment like it was yesterday. My oldest son, Taylor, was a high school junior playing football. He had only resumed playing the sport during his sophomore year, after skipping freshman football. He had been a multi-sport athlete for many years, playing soccer, baseball, basketball, and eventually football. He was a good athlete with every coach vying to get him to "focus" on their sport, but it was football that was quickly becoming his passion. When he got home from practice that day, he looked at me and said, "Dad, I think I'd like to play football in college."

All I remember thinking was, "OK. I don't know how this works, but we'll figure it out and see what opportunities exist for you." I quietly worried that he was too late... too slow... too small... that he wasn't academic enough for private schools or that we didn't have enough money. All the things a parent worries about.

So I'm guessing your son has told you that he's interested in playing college football. So what does that mean? What does he need to do? How will coaches find him? Where do you turn? This book is intended to help guide you in your shared quest for post high school athletic opportunities. My hope is that you will not just focus on the destination ("college football"), but that you will appreciate all that this process offers the both of you: opportunities for your son to develop independence, persistence, and self-confidence; the chance to strengthen your relationship; and an opportunity for you as a parent to guide your son in the transition to adulthood and to watch him take greater responsibility for his life.

Pursuing Post High School Football Opportunities

I like the expression "pursuing" post high school football opportunities better than "getting recruited", as I believe this paints a more realistic picture of what most people will experience. Few will be pursued… most athletes will have to be the pursuer. To that end, my first rule of this process is this:

The only person responsible for finding your son an opportunity to play college football is YOUR SON. It's not mom & dad's job, it's not your high school coach's job, nor is it a recruiting coordinator's job. It's HIS alone.

Yes, we need to be there to help guide, teach, encourage, and protect our sons. But, we also need to be there to watch over them as they struggle through the process and work toward a decision.

Additionally, the phrase "post high school football opportunities" better expresses the idea that there are LOTS of different opportunities and pathways to continuing to play the sport.

The ideal candidate to play college football is a very special person. They will embody many different qualities including not only athleticism, but intelligence, self-discipline, determination, enthusiasm, self-sufficiency and a strong work ethic.

The second rule follows the first:

The desire to be a college student-athlete needs to be the athlete's alone. This goal must be grounded in a deep passion for the game of football, the desire to get a college education, and a willingness to work extremely hard.

Regardless of whether you are a football player at a DII, DIII, or a big time DI program, you are going to be working extremely hard. DI programs require an almost year round commitment to training. The demands are much higher at this level than at other levels because of the pressure that comes with winning for coaching staffs and their administrations, but the reward is also much higher with having a full scholarship, state of the art facilities, and being able to play in front of 60,000+ fans week in and week out. DII and DIII programs tend to be more balanced with longer breaks away from school, but a typical day at any level will consist of rigorous off-season workouts, physical practices, and lots of film-room studying (per NCAA rules, Division II and Division III coaches can't require their players to stay over the summer for workouts, but often times it is strongly encouraged).

Incoming freshman players will be competing against older players, sometimes as much as six years older. Your teammates were likely the best players on their teams, in their conference, and in their state. Very often, lower level schools will have numerous players that have chosen to "drop down" from a higher level school in order to get more playing time. You can expect to be competing with four, six, or more players at your position, all of whom are likely stronger due to their years training and maturation. It is rare that a high school athlete walks on a college campus with enough skill, physical maturation, strength and knowledge to play immediately. For every level except for DIII, the redshirt year exists as a way to allow athletes time to mature physically and to get adjusted to the college rigors. If you possess the drive to play college football, then it is important that you understand the demands that will be placed on you along with the wide range of opportunities that exist and where you potentially fit.

A Day in the Life of a Student-Athlete
by Taylor Mitchell

Let's start by saying that a "normal" day as a collegiate football player is anything but normal. As soon as you show-up on campus for your first day of fall football camp, you will be fully immersed into the high demands of being a collegiate student-athlete. While fall camp isn't as physically demanding as it once was because of the physical limitations now imposed on practices, they are still long days full of football. An average day consists of meetings, film, walkthroughs and practices with extensive amounts of new terminology being thrown at new players. Fall camp can be extremely draining both physically and mentally, but this is just a glimpse into the long days to come once classes start.

During the season, student-athletes can expect to spend 10 hours or more on campus between classes, lifting, meetings, film and practice. There is limited social or free time during the season, but it is part of the fun of getting to know your teammates, especially those in your position group. To add to these long days, there is also the chance of missing class because of travel for road games. Depending on the level you are playing at and the conference you are playing in, you can expect to spend anywhere from 10 minutes to 24+ hours of travel for a single game (yes, there are some crosstown rivalries where there is little to no travel involved).

I played at a Division II school in a tough geographical location where travel for road games was extremely difficult. Our shortest trip of the season consisted of 16 hours on a bus, 8 hours in each direction, and this was the only game of the season where we left on a Friday for a Saturday game. For every other road football game, we would leave two days in advance of kickoff making the departure date on Thursday almost every week. I was a part of yearly trips that lasted 16+ hours one direction and even 24 hour trips back home after a Saturday game which put us back on campus late Sunday night (because of flights we would stay in hotels Saturday after the game and then travel all day Sunday).

While these trips were long, it is one of my most memorable experiences as a collegiate athlete. It was also just another component that my teammates and I accepted for being a student-athletes at the Division II level (which we referred to as the bus leagues). It would have been easy to use our long road trips as an excuse to do mediocre in school, but with proper time management and organization any student can be successful. I was able to juggle multiple jobs, serve on student government and participate on various committee's while in school. All this prepared me for life after football to handle the rigors and difficulties that life can throw at you.

Being a collegiate student-athlete requires a high level of commitment, a ton of hard work, endurance, and toughness. Bearing this in mind, it is a good idea for high school athletes to not commit to just one sport too early. Entering college with a high level of passion left for your sport is essential if you want to have a chance of competing at the next level.

College Football Opportunities

How Many Roster Spots Are Available?

2

      College football is played at multiple levels: DI-FBS, DI-FCS (formerly 1AA), Division II, Division III, Junior College, and NAIA. The amount of athletic scholarships available, the number of teams and roster spots varies by level.

Division I -FBS (Football Bowl Subdivision) – 130 teams (including three military academies) with 85 scholarships per team. Scholarships are full only and can't be split. FBS programs can only have 105 players participating in fall camp before the start of classes.

Division I -FBS (Military Academies) - The three military academies can recruit unlimited numbers of athletes, as every student receives a full scholarship. They utilize prep academies for players that need to transition into the rigorous academic environment of the service academies. These prep schools serve as "JV teams" and play actual games, but the player's athletic eligibility window (5 years to compete 4 years) does not start until they enter the Academy.

Division I -FCS (Football Championship Subdivision) – 125 teams, max 63 scholarships per team that can be divided among up to 85 athletes. Some conferences and schools restrict themselves to fewer than 63 or none. The Ivy (10 teams) and Pioneer (10 teams) Leagues do not offer football scholarships. The Patriot League used to offer no athletic scholarships, but has transitioned to 60 scholarships. FCS teams can only have 95 players participating in fall camp before the start of classes.

Division II – 171 schools offering a maximum of 36 scholarships divided among up to 85 athletes. Many schools and conferences offer less than 36 depending on funding at the school and conference rules.

Division III – 239 schools, none offer athletic scholarships, only academic scholarships. No redshirting. Student-athletes have 4 years to play 4.

NAIA – 88 Schools offering partial athletic scholarships. Student-athletes can redshirt.

Junior College – 133 teams offering nothing to some athletic scholarship; bear in mind that most junior colleges cost less than a traditional 4 year university.

Estimated Numbers of Available Scholarships

	Schools	Roster	Scholarships	Total Roster Spots	Total Scholarships
D1-FBS	127	105	85	13,335	10,795
Military	3	105	105	315	315
D1-FCS	105	95	63	9,975	6,615
D1-Ivy	20	95	0	1,900	0
D2	100	105	36	10,500	3,600
D2	71	105	20	7,455	1,420
D3	239	120	0	28,680	0
NAIA	88	105	20	9,240	1,760
Juco - CA	70	105	0	7,350	0
Juco - NJCAA	67	105	15	7,035	1,005
				95,785	**25,510**

*** DII is broken into two buckets simply to help estimate leagues and teams that are fully & partially funded** *Research done by National Football Foundation ("Number of colleges", 2016)

Approximately 50% of the football opportunities exist with NO athletic scholarship dollars whatsoever. Less than 20% of football players will receive a full athletic scholarship. The remaining 30% will receive only a partial athletic scholarship. The majority of the opportunities will exist at schools where academic standards are high and it is the only way to get admitted to the school. Therefore, it is incumbent on athletes to give themselves the most options by working hard on their academics.

Partial vs. Full Scholarship

At the DI-FBS level, a football player is either on full scholarship or no scholarship. At the DI-FCS, DII and NAIA levels, partial scholarships are the norm. At the partial scholarship schools, it's not uncommon for players to start on some type of a partial scholarship. In the seasons ahead, players that continue to move up the depth chart can see their scholarship increase over their 4 years, but this isn't always guaranteed. Top FCS recruits can be offered full scholarships, but this is more the exception than the norm. The implication is that the player is likely to play early and be a significant contributor.

At the DII, NAIA, and Junior College level, schools will typically offer some type of a dollar amount or an equivalent of some type of fixed cost (50% of tuition, 100% of tuition). Within DII, the first limitation on scholarships is established by the NCAA (max of 36) and the next by conference rules (i.e. conference establishes a 30 scholarship max). Additionally, each school will determine the level of funding that they can provide to their individual sports team. A school's budget may only give the equivalent of 15 scholarships to the football coach to allocate. Those 15 scholarships are equivalent to a full scholarship of an in-state student, say $20,000. This means that the coach has $300,000 in scholarship dollars to allocate to up to 85 football players each year.

This would be an average of $3,500 a year per player. At fully funded DII programs, the top scholarship offer is typically full tuition.

Along with football scholarships, some schools can use other forms of aid such as grants, tuition waivers and other forms of general scholarships to help provide aid to their student-athletes. Grant money is FREE money, just like scholarships, to those who qualify because of financial hardships, but this money does run out if you don't apply on time for the FAFSA.

It's important to note that at any of the partial scholarship schools, student-athletes can combine academic scholarships with athletic and financial aid. By working hard in school and doing well on standardized tests, you can help to reduce your college costs. This is important when you consider that 86% of the rosters opportunities will have you pay for some or all of your cost of attendance.

Who Am I Competing With?

How crowded is the field of "applicants" for these football roster spots? The National Federation of State High School Associations shows that 1.1 million boys played high school football in 2014-15. If you look at the typical class progression in a high school football program, the composition of the players is probably something like this:

Estimated Number High School Football Players By Grade

Grade	% of Total	# Players	
9th	35%	389,989	
10th	28%	311,991	
11th	21%	233,993	
12th	16%	178,280	*
		1,114,253	

Total # High School Football Players Per NFHS 2014-15 Survey

Est. Football Roster Spots Available to H.S. Freshman

	Schools	Est. Spots for Frosh (per team)	Total Spots for Frosh	% of High School Seniors
D1-FBS	127	22	2,794	1.6%
Military	3	40	120	0.1%
D1-FCS	105	25	2,625	1.5%
D1-Ivy	20	25	500	0.3%
D2	171	20	3,420	1.9%
D3	239	30	7,170	4.0%
NAIA	88	25	2,200	1.2%
Juco - CA	70	35	2,450	1.4%
Juco - NCJA	67	35	2,345	1.3%
			23,624	13.3%

*Research done by National Football Foundation ("Number of colleges", 2016)

Only the top 3% of high school football players can expect to receive a football opportunity at a DI-FCS or FBS school. In total, there are opportunities for roughly the top 13% of high school athletes and 40% of these opportunities will be based completely on academics!

Being a solid high school student athlete will increase your post high school football options by 66%!

The collegiate athletic landscape is extremely competitive. Regardless of the level of play, incoming freshman will be competing against older players that are sometimes as much as six years older. Every position will have three to six players competing for playing time and new players will arrive every year adding to the competition. At the lower levels of play, it can still be extremely competitive due to numerous players that opt to "drop down" from higher levels of play because of NCAA transfer rules. These are often players that have come to realize that they may never get significant, if any, playing time at their level of play and they make a decision to drop down to a level that is a better FIT for them.

I Want to Play College Football

What are my next steps?

3

You've made the decision to play college football, so where do you begin? You've already taken the first step, by setting a goal of playing college football. Next, you need to figure out where you are at athletically (self-assess) and determine a reasonably specific goal: "I want to try to play football at X level or XYZ School".

Here are some specific steps to take as you begin your pursuit of playing college football. Each of these will have a varying level of complexity and sub lists of things to do. Here's the broad list:

- Stay on top of your academics
  - Meet with your guidance counselor to make sure you are on a college preparatory path
  - Prepare for the standardized tests (ACT/SAT)
  - Take the ACT/SAT multiple times if necessary
  - Make sure you are meeting the NCAA requirements
- Continue to develop as an athlete
  - Work at your desired sport
  - Continue your training
  - Stay active with multiple sports
- Register with the NCAA Eligibility Center
- Apply for Financial Aid (the FAFSA) on time
- Meet with your high school football coach(s) to tell them of your desire to playing after high school
- Self-Assess – Identify your FIT

- Develop a list of schools that you're interested in pursuing
- Develop a marketing strategy
  - Communication
  - Unofficial visits
  - Camps

Having a Marketing Strategy
By Taylor Mitchell

Kids in high school have numerous tools at their disposal that they can utilize to get their highlight tapes and information in front of college football coaches with ease. I played high school football before the technological revolution of Hudl and social media where you can now simply highlight yourself online and send your tape to hundreds of coaches instantly. The process is so streamlined today that coaches EXPECT to find your tape on Hudl where less than ten years ago, players including myself would upload highlight tapes onto YouTube or burn DVD's to send our tape out to schools. There is NO reason for players to burn and send out DVD's any longer, keep it simple!

It's important to realize that coaches receive HUNDREDS of emails, text messages and phone calls a day so do not be discouraged when a coach does not get back to you immediately. With coaches being bombarded with potential recruits, it also means that you need to be able to capture the attention of these coaches however you can. If you're 6'8", every email you send out to coaches needs to have "6'8" OL from Washington" in the subject line. If you have a 4.0 GPA and you're emailing DIII coaches or prestigious academic institutions, you need to put this in the subject line. Understand what the coaches you are reaching out to are looking for in prospective student-athletes and sell how you fit these qualities.

With communication being so digitalized in today's society, it allows for recruits to connect and speak with coaches in numerous ways. *Every coach has an email, cell phone, office phone, and Twitter account. You can typically find a majority of a coaches contact information on their schools athletic website. When I went through the recruiting process, I was forced to pick-up the phone and cold call coaches. DON'T be afraid to call coaches. Players often times send the same generic messages via Twitter, email and text to every coach they can. Standout and be different, separate yourself from the rest of the recruits schools are looking at. I have seen players get offered official visits and eventually scholarships because they called a coach and were able to sell them on why they were a fit for the football program. Emails can get lost in the mix with coaches receiving hundreds of them a day. DON'T be surprised when you call and get a coach on the phone, be prepared with questions and your pitch, you may only get that coach on the phone once.*

When you are sending emails to coaches, be sure to keep them simple so that coaches can easily see the important information that will make you standout. Be sure to fill out the Subject Line of the email, address the coach you are emailing at the beginning of the email, introduce yourself, include things like your hometown, where you go to high school, your athletic vitals and your highlight tape.

Remember that the subject line is the first thing a coach sees and it is your first opportunity to standout and to sell yourself. I have received numerous emails with no subject lines or that are generic. The subject lines in the emails I receive far too often say something like, "Recruit for you" or "Checkout this Hudl Highlight video." As I mentioned earlier, give the coach a reason to open the email!

Some of you may be rolling your eyes reading these tips on sending emails thinking this is elementary, but for far too many high schoolers, it's foreign and most likely the first time they've sent emails before. There have been instances where student-athletes will simply email dozens to hundreds of separately and personalizing them. There is also an infinitely higher chance of a coach opening and responding to an email if it starts with a, "Coach Smith" rather than a generic, copy-and-pasted "Coach" at the beginning of the email.

When you are introducing yourself and giving your key vitals, keep it concise and simple. Remember, coaches are extremely busy and they're most likely going to skim the email and search for the important information and decide if they're going to watch your highlight tape or not. After you introduce yourself including mentioning where you're from and what High School you attend, it is okay and recommended that you list other key information like the positions you play, awards/accolades that you've received, your GPA/test scores, your stats and different athletic testing results like your 40 time and squat max if they are scores/times that will make you standout.

Finally, be sure to mention to the coach WHY you are interested in their football program. Coaches receive hundreds of generic emails a day with potential recruits telling every coach that they're "interested" in their program. Do your research before contacting coaches and make sure that their football program is going to be a good fit for you whether it is geographically, athletically or even academically. Make sure that it's a school worth traveling to, that they offer different degrees you may be interested in, that it's a football program you could see yourself playing for!

For many of you, these "simple" things seem like commonsense and are obvious, but as a coach, I have received very few emails that are personalized and a majority of them are considered spam sent to hundreds of coaches. When you get to college, you are going to learn quickly that "the little things matter." Treat your recruitment process the same way and make sure every coach has a reason to open up your mail!

The "Recruiting Process"

A Unique Job Search

4

The phrase "Recruiting Process" is broadly used to describe the experience that every high school student-athlete will go through as they pursue opportunities for college athletics. The reality is that very few athletes are recruited in the high profile manner of a top national prospect that is courted by the likes of Alabama, Ohio State, and USC. The majority of the 25,000 high school seniors that choose to continue to play collegiately will have to work hard to find their own path, to make connections with coaches and to decide on a school that best FITS them.

I always encouraged my sons to view the "Recruiting Process" as being more like a job search and a prolonged job interview. Every year college coaches will have 20+ "job openings" on their football team. Coaches are seeking the best candidates to fill those openings. Job seekers (student-athletes) are seeking the best FIT for themselves: a place where they can get their education and compete as an athlete. Their hope is to be productive, to get to play and to contribute to the team. Coaches are going to do extensive background checks on their prospective "employees", looking at their life resume and interviewing available references.

The "Recruiting Process" will be unique for EVERY student-athlete based on a multitude of factors. These can include your physical attributes like body build, athleticism, and maturation, location (large city or rural), knowledge/family experience with college athletics, financial resources, experience of your high school coach, level and types of colleges targeted, your high school playing experience, success in other sports, or having other college bound athletes on your team.

There are also tons of special circumstances that can occur with each athlete that can affect their "recruiting process". These should not be viewed as obstacles, but as purely elements that need to be accounted for as you develop your personal marketing plan. Some of these circumstances can be:

- Being a late bloomer, a player who physically develops late
- Playing behind or "out of position" because of a college prospect, your team's needs or an injury to another player
- Projecting to play a completely different position in college
- Playing as a specialist (kicker, punter, long snapper)
- An injury that limits or eliminates a season
- Targeting an academically specialized school in the Ivy or Patriot Leagues, a military academy or an engineering school like Colorado or South Dakota School of Mines
- Starting to play football late in high school
- Experiencing early academic troubles that correct
- Family circumstances that impact academics or athletic participation, like a move, health issues, divorce or a school change

Just as in life, there are many things that happen over which we have no control. The key to overcoming adversity is to focus on the things that we DO have control over, specifically our attitude, our effort, and our enthusiasm. When we acknowledge our circumstances and look honestly at them, we are able to develop a plan for dealing with them. This gives us the freedom to have a positive attitude and joy despite our circumstances. These are the qualities that coaches and employers are looking for in prospective athletes or employees. People that are resilient, positive and aren't deterred by challenges will all make great teammates and co-workers one day.

Mail, Letters, & School Information

A school sent me mail or an email, what does it mean?

NCAA rules allow DI football programs to send materials & letters in the mail beginning Sept 1 of a recruit's junior year. DII schools can begin to send materials on June 15 at the end of a recruit's sophomore year. DIII schools can send materials to any high school aged athlete.

There are some basic types of documents that prospects might receive in the mail and each can give some insight into their recruitment. The first is generic literature about the university or the football program. Some schools will send promotional materials about their coaches, facilities, or achievements. Programs that have significant recruiting budgets will reach out to hundreds of prospects, casting a wide net. Consider this simply a compliment like "you're cute", but it's not a marriage proposal. It means that you are on their radar screen.

Next, many programs will send out information on their high school summer camps. Again, this is casting a wide net to hopefully draw hundreds of prospects to their camp with the hopes of finding one or two "keepers". (Note we discuss Summer Camps in a later chapter). Lastly and most importantly, any type of letter that is written specifically to you is a sign of at least a greater level of interest. What does the letter say? Is it generic in nature? In most cases, it will be something like, "we have identified you as a prospective student-athlete. We will be watching you in the coming months." A handwritten note is even more significant. If the letter instructs you to complete the recruiting questionnaire, email the coach, or give them a phone call, then make sure you do it.

Mail Coming In
By Taylor Mitchell

I remember being a senior in high school when my younger brother Josh had his first college football recruiting letter arrive at our high school. It was a large packet with a giant "A" on the front of it, the University of Alabama. Was Alabama recruiting him? Was he going to get an offer? What do these letters mean? I remember the initial excitement we all had when his first letter came in, but we were uneducated, naïve, and had no idea what it meant.

After having an All-League Junior season in a perennial power conference in the state of Washington, Alabama was simply casting their net for potential recruits around the country. It certainly captured his attention and got him excited about their football program which meant that their recruiting department did a great job in sending proper marketing materials out. Like Josh, there were most likely hundreds of other potential student-athletes that were fired-up about playing for the Crimson Tide. This was an example of "generic" or spam mail being sent out.

My youngest brother Caleb also received a letter from the University of Alabama, but it was regarding their summer prospect camp for specialists. This letter left him wondering if he had the athletic potential to receive a scholarship or to be a potential recruit for their program or if this piece of mail was simply sent out to every specialist in the country similar to Josh's piece of mail. He took the time to email one of their coaches and found out that there was interest and that they wanted to watch him workout in-person. Like marketing materials that are sent out, summer camp letters can be sent out to hundreds of potential recruits. Do your research by seeing if the school already has commitments at your position for your or reach out to a coach to see if they are truly interested in you.

As a programs interest grows toward a potential student-athlete, the mail will begin to come in more frequently and will become more personal of nature. With athletic departments and football support staffs growing in numbers, recruiting departments have been able to get more creative in the content that they are able to send out to recruits. This can include photo shopped content of a recruit playing at their school among other materials to create "buzz" and to get a prospect intrigued about playing for their program.

Handwritten letters are another form of "personal" content that can be sent out and shows how serious coaches are about you as a potential recruit. Typically handwritten notes will come in the mail if you have an offer or if you are high on that particular school's recruiting board meaning an offer could be imminent.

In a time where a majority of communication has become digitized via email, social media, and text messaging, handwritten notes are VERY special and should be treated as such. Both of my brothers Josh and Nick who were sought out and recruited by Division I programs received frequent handwritten notes from teams that had offered them, but coaches at all levels will send these letters if there is serious interest.

What is an "Offer?"

The word "offer" is used regularly in the world of recruiting and it can have many meanings. Let's clarify the most basic meaning of the word, its implications/guarantees, and the different types of offers.

The word "offer" is generally meant to describe a verbal offer that is nonbinding by a College or University for a position on the football team. YOU MUST GET THE COACH TO CLARIFY exactly what they are "offering". Is it an athletic scholarship (full or partial), a "preferred walk-on", or simply a position on the team? It is also important to keep in mind that these scholarship offers and financial aid agreements are for only one year and are renewed at the discretion of the head football coach.

If a DI-FBS school is offering a scholarship, it can ONLY be a FULL athletic scholarship. If the school is a DI-FCS, DII or NAIA school, they can be offering a full, partial or simply a "preferred walk-on" roster spot. Again, it is up to the player to find out WHAT IS BEING OFFERED.

For schools that divide scholarships up, there may not be a concrete answer as to how much your offer is going to be until you are closer to signing day. The recruiting game is also a numbers game. Every coach and school is trying to maximize their money for the quality of player they are getting. As other players make their commitments, it can either relieve money or tie up money that would otherwise go to you. Be sure to keep your options open until you have a clear answer as to what your financial situation is going to be.

A Preferred Walk-On position provides no athletic financial aid, but it does guarantee a player a roster spot on a football team. There is the potential of a walk-on earning scholarship money as it becomes available through attrition and as they progress through their careers, but there is no guarantee of this happening and is usually special when it occurs. DI-FBS, DI-FCS, and DII programs are limited in the number of athletes they can have on their roster for Title IX and financial reasons. DIII schools can't offer athletic scholarships, but they do actively recruit and try to get players to "commit" to play for their team. It is not uncommon for top tier DIII programs to have over 120 players on the roster, some over 150.

Additionally, some DIII programs will field a JV team. Players need to evaluate roster information as part of their decision process.

What is a "Commitment?"

When a player tells a coach that he is accepting an "offer" (scholarship or walk-on), he is making a VERBAL commitment. Nothing is signed and nothing is binding. It is a verbal agreement only. In most states, people under the age of 18 are not allowed to enter into contracts or agreements without the consent of a responsible adult (i.e. a parent or guardian). This is because they lack the life experience and maturity necessary to make a long term decision.

Families and players need to be cautious in making a "commitment" too easily. Making and breaking a commitment whimsically like a young person getting into and out of dating relationships is not the way to open doors for your future. Adults (parents, guardians, and coaches) should provide structure, perspective and rational input to young people as they look for a college home.

There are advantages to committing early. First and most importantly, it assures the player of having a place to play their sport. Second, it ends the possible chaos of being recruited and the stress of making a decision. Remember, schools set goals of signing a certain number of players for a specific position in a recruiting class (we want 3 linebackers). To make sure they sign their 3 players, the school will target as many as 6 to 10 players that they feel fit their profile. Therefore, it is logical that the first 3 players to make a verbal commitment will fill their quota. Very often, schools will stop recruiting the other players for these roster spots. There are always exceptions to rules, as some schools will continue to recruit a truly extraordinary athlete figuring if they commit, that they will move a player to another position or a lesser player may opt to go elsewhere knowing that are likely going to be further down the depth chart. Players can also be dropped or told they no long have an offer from that particular school if better players commit.

NOTE: Players and families need to understand that a school's "offer" is also a verbal agreement with nothing binding to them. Schools take their time in doing their research before they offer a student-athlete, as they know that extending an "offer" is a serious commitment of their resources and reputation. Reneging on an offer would not reflect well on them, therefore they take their time before they make an offer. Athletes should follow this same rule, take your time and make a sound decision. Emotions, hype, and happy feelings are not going to help you get up at 5 am for off-season workouts.

The "Recruiting Process" can help to prepare your son for the competitive environment of college athletics or the workforce. Viewing this process like a competitive job search will help everyone keep things in perspective.

Academic Requirements

Eligibility for Admission and Competition

5

High school students have multiple academic hurdles to clear in order to participate in college athletics:

1. Graduate high school
2. Get "Cleared" by the NCAA or NAIA Eligibility Center
3. Get Admitted to the college or university

These requirements aren't perfectly synchronous, so the student-athlete and his family have to stay vigilant to make sure all requirements are addressed.

NCAA or NAIA Eligibility Center

Students can go to the NCAA or NAIA Eligibility Center website and register starting as early as the beginning of their sophomore year. This isn't required for DIII or JuCo's. The eligibility center helps student athletes to see the academic requirements and standardized test scores needed to be deemed "eligible" by the respective associations.

Academic Requirements

There are different academic requirements based on the level of school that is being pursued within the NCAA: Division I, Division II, and Division III. The NAIA is a separate governing body for colleges, just like the NCAA, that sets its own standards for eligibility. Junior Colleges are governed by their respective associations (NJCAA, CCAAA). Their general purpose is to help non-qualifying student-athletes to obtain an associate's degree and move on to a 4 year school.

The NCAA establishes basic standards that student-athletes must meet to be deemed "Academically Eligible" to play at any Division I or II School. Because Division III schools do not provide athletic aid, the NCAA does not establish the academic requirements for athletically eligibility. Division III schools tend to be small, private institutions and are generally more expensive than public schools. Academic requirements for admission are established by each school and are generally more rigorous than public schools.

In 2016, the NCAA introduced more stringent requirements for athletic eligibility to become a qualifier (eligible to compete). In addition, they introduced the "Academic Redshirt" for partial qualifiers that allow for the student-athlete to receive an athletic scholarship and practice with the team, but they aren't eligible for game competition. This was done as a means of allowing the student-athlete time to acclimate to the academic and athletic demands of college.

GPA and Standardized Test Scores

Academic requirements by the NCAA have become more rigorous over the last few years. The NCAA establishes higher eligibility standards for Division I schools versus Division II schools. A minimum grade point average (GPA) is calculated using grades just from "core classes", classes that are required for academic eligibility (see below). The core GPA is combined with standardized test scores on a sliding scale grid to determine the minimum GPA and test score required. The lower the GPA, the higher the standardized test scores required. The higher the GPA, the lower the test scores.

ACT/SAT Scores must be submitted directly to the NCAA Eligibility Center. You simply add the Eligibility Center (code 9999) to the list of schools that you want to report your scores.

If you are unsure what classes you have taken may be considered "core classes" you can simply go to http://www.ncaa.org/student-athletes/future/core-courses to check and see. Once you get to this home page you simply click on the "Find your high school's list of NCAA courses" and then search for your high school.

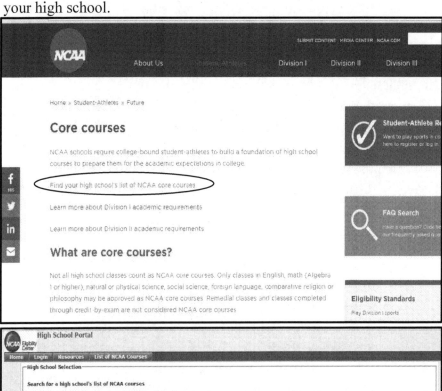

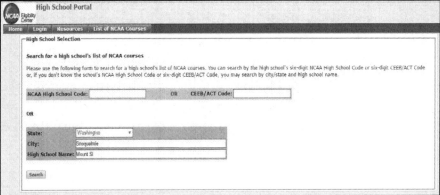

Once you select your high school, you can view each subject area that is considered a "core course" and from there you can make sure that you have been taking the appropriate courses. Lower level remedial courses and classes completed through credit-by-exam are NOT considered core courses. Students do have the opportunity to retake courses for GPA repair work and the higher of the two grades will be counted.

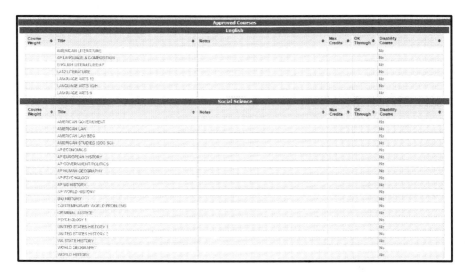

Division I Requirements

Core-Course requirements:

- 4 years of English
- 3 years of Math (Algebra 1 or higher)
- 2 years of natural/physical science (1 year of a lab, if offered)
- 1 year of additional English, math or natural/physical science
- 2 years of social science
- 4 years of additional courses (any area above, foreign language or comparative religion/philosophy)

Qualifier Requirements

- 16 core courses
    - o 10 completed before the start of seventh semester. Seven of the ten must be in English, math or natural/physical science
        - ▪ "Locked in" for core-course GPA calculation
- Corresponding test score (ACT sum score or SAT combined score) and core-course GPA (minimum 2.300) on Sliding Scale
- Graduate from high school

Academic Redshirt Requirements

- 16 core courses
    - o No grades/credits "locked in" (repeated course after the seventh semester begins may be used for initial eligibility).
- Corresponding test score (ACT sum score or SAT combined score) and core-course GPA (minimum 2.0) on Sliding Scale
- Graduate from high school

Division II Initial Eligibility Requirements

Core-Course requirements:

- 3 years of English
- 2 years of Math (Algebra 1 or higher)
- 2 years of natural/physical science (1 year of a lab, if offered)
- 3 years of additional English, math or natural/physical science
- 2 years of social science

- 4 years of additional courses (any area above, foreign language or comparative religion/philosophy)

Test Scores

- Required minimum SAT score of 820 or an ACT sum score of 68
  - Beginning August 1, 2018, Division II will also use a sliding scale to match test scores and core-course GPA
    - SAT scores used will be only the critical reading and math sections
    - ACT score used will be the sum of these 4 sections: English, math, reading, and science

Grade Point Average

- 2.0 minimum in Core Classes only
  - Beginning August 1, 2018, Division II will require a 2.20 core GPA
    - A 2.0 core GPA will be deemed a "Partial DII Qualifier" and the player will be an "Academic Redshirt"

Academic GPA Worksheet:

Also found on the NCAA Core Courses home page are both a Division I and II worksheet that can be used to calculate a student's core course GPA if there are any difficulties in doing so. There is an example of these worksheets below and you can see how easy it can be to calculate your core GPA if it isn't listed on your transcript.

Division I Worksheet

This worksheet is provided to assist you in monitoring your progress in meeting NCAA initial-eligibility standards. The NCAA Eligibility Center will determine your academic status after you graduate. Remember to check your high school's list of NCAA-approved courses for the classes you have taken.

Use the following scale: A = 4 quality points; B = 3 quality points; C = 2 quality points; D = 1 quality point.

English (4 years required)

10/7	Course Title	Credit	X	Grade	=	Quality Points (multiply credit by grade)
✓	Example: English 9	.5		A		(.5 x 4) = 2
	Total English Units					Total Quality Points

Mathematics (3 years required)

10/7	Course Title	Credit	X	Grade	=	Quality Points (multiply credit by grade)
	Example: Algebra 1	1.0		B		(1.0 x 3) = 3
	Total Mathematics Units					Total Quality Points

Natural/physical science (2 years required)

10/7	Course Title	Credit	X	Grade	=	Quality Points (multiply credit by grade)
	Total Natural/Physical Science Units					Total Quality Points

Additional year in English, mathematics or natural/physical science (1 year required)

10/7	Course Title	Credit	X	Grade	=	Quality Points (multiply credit by grade)
	Total Additional Units					Total Quality Points

Social science (2 years required)

10/7	Course Title	Credit	X	Grade	=	Quality Points (multiply credit by grade)
	Total Social Science Units					Total Quality Points

Additional academic courses (4 years required)

10/7	Course Title	Credit	X	Grade	=	Quality Points (multiply credit by grade)
Total	Total Additional Academic Units					Total Quality Points
	Total Quality Points from each subject area / Total Credits = Core-Course GPA		/		=	
		Quality Points	/	Credits	=	Core-Course GPA

Core-Course GPA (16 required) Beginning August 1, 2016, 10 core courses must be completed before the seventh semester and seven of the 10 must be a combination of English, math or natural or physical science for competition purposes. Grades and credits may be earned at any time for academic redshirt purposes.

Division II Worksheet

This worksheet is provided to assist you in monitoring your progress in meeting NCAA initial-eligibility standards. The NCAA Eligibility Center will determine your academic status after you graduate. Remember to check your high school's list of NCAA-approved courses for the classes you have taken.

Use the following scale: A = 4 quality points; B = 3 quality points; C = 2 quality points; D = 1 quality point.

English (3 years required)

Course Title	Credit	X	Grade	=	Quality Points (multiply credit by grade)
Example: English 9	.5		A		(.5 x 4) = 2
Total English Units					Total Quality Points

Mathematics (2 years required)

Course Title	Credit	X	Grade	=	Quality Points (multiply credit by grade)
Example: Algebra 1	1.0		B		(1.0 x 3) = 3
Total Mathematics Units					Total Quality Points

Natural/physical science (2 years required)

Course Title	Credit	X	Grade	=	Quality Points (multiply credit by grade)
Total Natural/Physical Science Units					Total Quality Points

Additional years in English, math or natural/physical science (3 years required)

Course Title	Credit	X	Grade	=	Quality Points (multiply credit by grade)
Total Additional Units					Total Quality Points

Social science (2 years required)

Course Title	Credit	X	Grade	=	Quality Points (multiply credit by grade)
Total Social Science Units					Total Quality Points

Additional academic courses (4 years required)

Course Title	Credit	X	Grade	=	Quality Points (multiply credit by grade)
Total Additional Academic Units					Total Quality Points
Total Quality Points from each subject area / Total Credits = Core-Course GPA		/		=	
	Quality Points	/	Credits	=	Core-Course GPA

NCAA Sliding Scale:

On the NCAA website, student-athletes can find a "Sliding Scale" which is used by the NCAA to determine if an athlete is going to be a qualifier. Student-athletes simply look for their GPA along with the necessary test score to determine if they are going to be a full, partial or non-qualifier. The sliding scale is shown below and can also be found online at the NCAA eligibility center.

Sliding Scale B Use for Division I beginning August 1, 2016		
NCAA DIVISION I SLIDING SCALE		
Core GPA	SAT Verbal and Math ONLY	ACT Sum
3.550	400	37
3.525	410	38
3.500	420	39
3.475	430	40
3.450	440	41
3.425	450	41
3.400	460	42
3.375	470	42
3.350	480	43
3.325	490	44
3.300	500	44
3.275	510	45
3.250	520	46
3.225	530	46
3.200	540	47
3.175	550	47
3.150	560	48
3.125	570	49
3.100	580	49
3.075	590	50
3.050	600	50
3.025	610	51
3.000	620	52
2.975	630	52
2.950	640	53
2.925	650	53
2.900	660	54
2.875	670	55
2.850	680	56
2.825	690	56
2.800	700	57
2.775	710	58
2.750	720	59
2.725	730	60
2.700	740	61
2.675	750	61
2.650	760	62
2.625	770	63
2.600	780	64
2.575	790	65
2.550	800	66
2.525	810	67
2.500	820	68
2.475	830	69
2.450	840	70
2.425	850	70
2.400	860	71
2.375	870	72
2.350	880	73
2.325	890	74
2.300	900	75
2.299	910	76
2.275	910	76
2.250	920	77
2.225	930	78
2.200	940	79
2.175	950	80
2.150	960	81
2.125	970	82
2.100	980	83
2.075	990	84
2.050	1000	85
2.025	1010	86
2.000	1020	86

DIVISION II COMPETITION SLIDING SCALE		
Use for Division II beginning August 1, 2018		
Core GPA	SAT (Verbal and Math ONLY)	ACT Sum
3.300 & above	400	37
3.275	410	38
3.250	420	39
3.225	430	40
3.200	440	41
3.175	450	41
3.150	460	42
3.125	470	42
3.100	480	43
3.075	490	44
3.050	500	44
3.025	510	45
3.000	520	46
2.975	530	46
2.950	540	47
2.925	550	47
2.900	560	48
2.875	570	49
2.850	580	49
2.825	590	50
2.800	600	50
2.775	610	51
2.750	620	52
2.725	630	52
2.700	640	53
2.675	650	53
2.650	660	54
2.625	670	55
2.600	680	56
2.575	690	56
2.550	700	57
2.525	710	58
2.500	720	59
2.475	730	60
2.450	740	61
2.425	750	61
2.400	760	62
2.375	770	63
2.350	780	64
2.325	790	65
2.300	800	66
2.275	810	67
2.250	820	68
2.225	830	69
2.200	840 & above	70 & above

DIVISION II PARTIAL QUALIFIER SLIDING SCALE		
Use for Division II beginning August 1, 2018		
Core GPA	SAT (Verbal and Math ONLY)	ACT Sum
3.050 & above	400	37
3.025	410	38
3.000	420	39
2.975	430	40
2.950	440	41
2.925	450	41
2.900	460	42
2.875	470	42
2.850	480	43
2.825	490	44
2.800	500	44
2.775	510	45
2.750	520	46
2.725	530	46
2.700	540	47
2.675	550	47
2.650	560	48
2.625	570	49
2.600	580	49
2.575	590	50
2.550	600	50
2.525	610	51
2.500	620	52
2.475	630	52
2.450	640	53
2.425	650	53
2.400	660	54
2.375	670	55
2.350	680	56
2.325	690	56
2.300	700	57
2.275	710	58
2.250	720	59
2.225	730	60
2.200	740	61
2.175	750	61
2.150	760	62
2.125	770	63
2.100	780	64
2.075	790	65
2.050	800	66
2.025	810	67
2.000	820 & above	68 & above

I spoke with a parent who lamented his family's missed opportunity at lowering the cost of college. Their son ended up playing at a prestigious Division III college. He was a very good student with an excellent grade point average. This did provide him with a generous academic scholarship, but his standardized test scores were pretty average. The dad said that he wished his family had invested time in SAT prep classes as it likely could've saved them another $20,000. Remember, YOUR ACADEMICS MATTER likely more than your athletic ability. Ultimately, you will be using your education to provide for yourself and your family. Make for a better tomorrow, by working hard today to be the best student that you can be.

Meet With Your High School Coach

Seek Help & Network

6

At the first opportunity, you will want to sit down with your head coach and your position coach to talk about your desire to play football after high school. Ask your coaches some of these questions:

- Do you think I can play after high school?
- What position(s) do I likely project at the college level?
- What level of schools should I pursue? Where do I fit?
- What are things that I should work on? What can I do better?
- Can you recommend some coaches or schools that I should contact?
- What are your recommendations or advice for me?

After you ask these questions, make sure you listen to what they have to say. Your coaches know you well and their passion is helping their players to reach their fullest potential. Your coaches are also most likely former players, who may have contacts within college football programs. Additionally, college coaches value the feedback and opinions of your coaches. You could not ask for a better advocate.

Ask your head coach if he wants you to give out his name and contact information to college coaches. In some instances, he may want your position coach to be the lead person talking with schools.

*Make sure you take the time **to write down** the advice, guidance and suggestions that your coaches give you. With them written down, it is easier to make sure you DO the things that they advise! Seize every opportunity to make yourself better!*

Network with Other Players

Reach out to former teammates or athletes that you know that are playing college football. If you are being recruited by schools and you know students or athletes at those schools, reach out to them. If not, ask the coach if he could get you the phone numbers of another athlete that you could speak to. Ask them questions about the school, the coaches, and the off-season program. Do they feel supported? What suggestions do they have for you? What things should you be looking for in other schools?

Networking is everything
By Taylor Mitchell

Throughout my younger brother's and my personal recruitment, we learned how powerful of a tool networking can be. The football profession is a very small, tight-knit community. I learned this early-on when I received my first scholarship offer from Humboldt State University. At Humboldt, I had a former high school teammate playing there at the time and the Head Coach and Offensive Coordinator had coached at the alma mater of my high school Head Coach and Defensive Coordinator. With these connections, I was able to talk to a current student-athlete about the football program and school, while having my coach's reach out to their coaches as references about possibly giving me an opportunity to play at Humboldt.

Even with the best references in the world, you still have to have great film, be a great citizen and achieve at a high level in the classroom, but having people vouch for your abilities is a big deal. College sports is ultimately a business and coaches want the best players they can get on their teams. My younger brother, Josh, was able to receive his first offer because his Offensive Line coach who was also a former National Football League player, reached out to then Oregon State head football coach Mike Riley who he had previously played for. He was already receiving other Division I interest, but this connection and phone call is what ultimately led to his first offer.

It's not very usual, but with Nick having an older brother already playing in a Division I football program, made his recruitment process much smoother because the coaches already knew of him. Through the recruitment of Josh, the Oregon State coaches were also able to get to know Nick as well. Having connections at programs won't always guarantee a scholarship, but a coach's word can go a long ways.

While networking paid dividends for my recruitment, there are also thousands of athletes that will be recruited and offered by schools where there are no prior connections between coaches. As a college football Recruiting Coordinator, it is imperative for me to do all of the research that I can do and a positive word from a high school coach can be a slam dunk for a recruit. Colleges and Universities are looking to invest thousands of dollars into a young adult and they want to make sure they're doing so in the right person.

College coaches ultimately want the best players that they can get and a conversation between your high school coach and a college coach is inevitable. Make sure your high school coach has nothing but great things to say about you.

Self-Assess

Be Honest With Yourself and Others
7

Self-awareness happens as part of the maturation process. It is recognizing how I stack up against others, an awareness of my strengths and weaknesses. It is the ability to look objectively at myself. With this awareness, I can choose to work hard at improving my weaknesses. I can decide to no longer pursue certain activities because of my lack of skill or I can choose to focus on my strengths. Self-awareness enables me to set realistic goals that are both challenging and achievable.

College coaches are accustomed to prospects regularly "fudging" on different aspects of themselves. A Division I recruiting coordinator used to keep a height measuring strip on the inside of his office door. He made it a point of staying at his desk when recruits would come to visit. This way he made sure that every player would have to come through his doorway, allowing him to gauge their actual height.

Another technique coach's use is to encourage players to take pictures with them after a visit. Players enjoy posting pictures on social media making it a great form of publicity for that football program and coaches get to see how their prospect stacks up size wise next to one of their coaches.

Longtime Division II head football coach Rob Smith often referenced the "2-2-2 Rule" in the recruiting process. He was telling his recruiting coordinators to subtract 2 inches from the height, add 2 tenths of second to their forty time, and subtract 2 tenths from the grade point average of whatever their prospective student-athletes list on their profile or emails.

You fudge by saying that you are 6'1", when you are really 5'11". Or saying that you run a 4.50 second 40 yard dash, when you really run it in 4.70 seconds. Exaggerating on your grades, when you will eventually have to show your transcript. A big reason that coaches get out and visit prospects in person during the evaluation period, is so they can "eyeball" prospects and confirm their physical attributes for themselves. What's more refreshing for a coach than to find out that you are "the real deal", just who you said you were. Nothing more, nothing less. The worst thing you can do is to burn a bridge with a coach by lying about yourself. If you don't fit a certain school or level of school, it is possible that a coach could speak to another coaching friend at a school where you might be a better fit. The coaching world is very small and tightly connected. Don't create your own obstacles.

The faster you take a realistic look at yourself and embrace WHO YOU ARE, the faster you can identify schools where you have the best FIT. In doing this, you can help to make sure you get the first shot at the available roster spots at the schools you are most interested in attending.

Physical Attributes

There are aspects of who we are that are out of our control. Your physical attributes have everything to do with genetics. Your body frame, bone density, muscle composition, as well as height and weight are dictated by factors beyond your control. Some attributes can be enhanced and improved upon through training and practice, but with limits. Aspects like how fast you are, how high you can jump, how quickly you can change direction, and your general coordination can be improved. Someone who can run the 100 meter dash in 12 seconds could improve to 11.7 seconds with lots of training, but they aren't going to run it in around 10 seconds like world class sprinters do.

Some people's bodies just do not allow them the necessary flexibility to be able to compete at the highest level. Chronic tight muscles that don't allow someone to touch their toes or inflexible hips that won't allow a rapid change in direction are not qualities of most successful college football players.

In football, there are certain physical qualities that must exist for one to compete at specific positions. Generally tall, large men will play on the offensive and defensive lines. Fast, skinny athletes will generally play at the skill positions of wide receiver and defensive backs. Short, fast, and shifty athletes will play running back. Lengthy, thick, and fast athletes will play at the linebacker position. Very tall, athletic players that don't have enough girth to play offensive line can play tight end. Players with a strong throwing arm will play quarterback and those with strong legs will play kicker. There can be exceptions to every rule, but players that don't fit the "typical" mold for a position will generally possess some qualities that compensate for their deficiencies. A shorter offensive lineman could possess adequate weight, but great athleticism and strength. A short skinny player could possess tremendous vertical speed.

Imagine a 6'5" player competing against a shorter 6' player. The 6'5" player is blocking the shorter player, trying to prevent him from getting past. The taller player's reach would allow him to put his hands on the shorter player without that player being able to reach and prevent him. Next, imagine a 350 pound player pushing against a 250 pound player. The larger player would have a significant advantage versus a smaller player. For these reasons, physical attributes make a significant difference and it is why coaches look for these qualities when they are recruiting.

Look at rosters of college football teams at all levels. Compare your height, weight, and speed to current players on college football rosters or to those that have just signed with college teams. How do you compare? Look at lists of recruits in this year's signing class at different levels of schools and compare yourself to them. Compare yourself to teammates or local players that are heading on to play collegiately. This can help you gauge yourself a little more realistically, which will help you identify schools where you are more likely to FIT.

Common Traits of College Athletes

If you click on the biographies of players on college football rosters, you will see lots of very accomplished, competitive and driven people. Look at their high school accolades, accomplishments and statistics. Most were leaders on their high school teams, a team captain and a campus or community leader. Very often these players played on the Varsity team as a sophomore. Many excelled at multiple sports. They were likely always one of the best athletes on their teams, regardless of the sport. They were probably "THE MAN" when they played youth sports. They were likely bigger, faster, and stronger than their peers earlier in life, as well throughout their high school years.

Each sports has an affinity to certain physical attributes. Basketball and volleyball favor height and jumping ability. Baseball players tend to have a strong arm and or quick hand eye coordination. Soccer goalies tend to be very tall and athletic, while all other soccer players will possess speed and endurance. Track favors speed and jumping ability. Football generally favors size, speed, and strength.

Lastly, college athletes are likely to be extremely competitive and driven people. They have probably been called too competitive or a sore loser more than once in their lifetime. Their resumes resemble those of "Type A" personalities with lots of activities, accomplishments, awards, and accolades. These qualities will serve them well and will help them thrive in the competitive landscape of college athletics.

What Does a DI Player Look Like?

- Large, physically advanced
- Fast, extremely athletic
- Early Varsity playing time (sophomore)
- Multi-sport star
- All-Conference standout by Sophomore or Junior season
- Generally regarded as the best athlete on every team they play on
- Schools will look for players that fit within a grid
  - O-Linemen – 6'3" to 6'9"
  - D-Linemen – 6' to 6' 5"
  - Quarterbacks – 6'2"+
  - Running Backs – 5'9"+
  - Linebackers – 6'2"+
  - DB's – 6'+

Schools at the highest level will go for the most physically developed and ready to play athletes. Middle and lower tier schools are accustomed to finding players that aren't as physically developed (underweight), using a redshirt year and developing them. There are obviously exceptions for some players as there are some teams that will pull the trigger in offering an undersized DB or RB with exceptional skills, but a majority of players will fit these molds.

What Do DII & DIII Players Look Like?

Typically smaller in size, shorter, less physically developed or ready to play as the DI athletes. Sometimes they have the size and weight characteristics, but they lack the athleticism or speed of DI players. Regardless, we are still talking about the top 10% of all high school football players, so this is still a very elite group.

DIII schools get lots of undersized, but hard working athletes.

- Linebacker/athletes that are well under 6'
- O-linemen that are 6' tall or 6'3
- DBs and WRs that are under 5'10"

Myth: Lower Levels of Play are Less Competitive

There is a HUGE misperception that the lower the level of play, the less competitive the game. Recognize that every level of play has some type of playoff and championship. At every level besides the DI-FBS, there is an extensive playoff tournament conducted to determine a National Champion. Every level of play will have athletes that have worked hard for three or more years to reach their senior season. On every team, at every level of play, only the best players will play. Almost every lower level team will have players that have chosen to "drop down" to play at a lower level for various reasons.

"The 'Big Time' is where you are."
Frosty Westering – DIII Pacific Lutheran Football Coach
300+ career wins, 3 time National Champion

Consider the following:

- Top DI-FCS programs regularly beat DI-FBS teams
- Top DII programs regularly defeat DI-FCS teams
- Top DIII programs regularly defeat DII teams
- In 2013, 11 DI-FCS teams beat DI-FBS teams
- In 2011, DII Humboldt State beat DI-FCS Cal Davis
  - Later that season, DI-FCS Cal Davis beat Sac State

- o Earlier that season, DI-FCS Sacrament State defeated Oregon State
- o In that season, Oregon State defeated the University of Washington
- o Humboldt > Cal Davis > Sac State > Oregon State > Washington

- Therefore, by the Transitive Property:
  - o DII Humboldt State should be able to defeat the University of Washington

Things are not this simple, but the point is that there is extremely competitive football to be played at EVERY level. Every team will have one or two elite players. Every year there are players signed or drafted into the NFL from lower levels of play. Sometimes good players grow or develop while they are in college. Sometimes players start playing the game later in life or an injury happens that causes them to be overlooked. If a player desires to play after high school, there are opportunities for those with the passion and the willingness to work hard.

Determine Your FIT

Finding the Right School & Level of Play

10

The first element of FIT is all about your Academics. Can you qualify to play for a NCAA DI or DII program? If qualifying is going to be an issue, then a Junior College is your only option. Are you more interested in attending a small college or a large university? Is an Ivy, Pioneer or Patriot League school more of what you are looking for? Do you want to pursue a military academy? These questions will help determine where you start.

The next element is to determine the right level of play. After talking with your coach, studying college rosters and comparing yourself to current and college bound players, you need to gauge where you FIT athletically. What type of high school player are you? A difference maker or a great teammate? Did you play Varsity early in your high school career? Are you a multi-sport star? Are you physically limited or physically mature?

Now focus on determining which level of play will provide you with the best experience that you are pursuing. Is your goal to be a walk-on at your "dream" school or at the highest level of play possible? Will you be happy serving as a scout team player for 5 years with that "dream school"? Will that be fulfilling for you? Are you interested in a unique academic centered athletic experience at an Ivy League school or a military academy? Do you want to be one of the better athletes on your FCS Championship contending team, rather than just another player at a lower level DI school? Does a smaller college setting at a DIII school appeal to you? Would you like to have a more "balanced" college experience? Being able to do a semester abroad, work at summer internships or play multiple sports in college? If so, then a DII, DIII or NAIA school might be the right fit. Answering these questions will help you to better define your target schools and then develop a targeted marketing plan.

Research Schools

Each school's website will provide you a wealth of information about the campus, student body, available majors and surrounding community. If you have the ability to visit campuses, you should do so. School visits are a critical way for you to see if the campus setting "feels right" for you. Is this somewhere you could see yourself for the next 4 or 5 years? What if football ended, would this still be a good fit? The statistics say that 50% of players stop playing the game due to injury or burnout.

"My encouragement to high school athletes is to look for schools that they would feel good attending if they were no longer playing football."

Wayne Lewis - Mount Si High School
Defensive Coordinator (WA)

Analyze the cost of attending all of the schools. Remember, that in most cases, you will receive little to no athletic scholarship. Look at your potential to receive academic scholarships or out of state waivers based on your grades and standardized test scores. Weigh the financial considerations in light of your family's circumstances and budget.

Retention of College Football Players
By Taylor Mitchell

While a majority, if not all kids, have a true love for the game of football, something changes through their years in college. A majority of student-athletes who sign a National Letter of Intent (NLI) will end their playing careers before their eligibility runs out or will transfer away from the school that they had originally signed with. Yes, you read that right. A majority of

---

college student-athletes DO NOT finish their playing careers at the school they originally signed with and it's not even close. A large majority of these kids either elect to retire because of injuries, have a lack of desire of continuing to play, or they elect to finish their careers at other schools.

The best advice I ever received going through the recruiting process was from my high school defensive coordinator Wayne Lewis who told me to make sure that I go to a school where I could see myself finishing school even if I stopped playing football. At the time, I thought there was NO way I would ever stop playing and that my love for the game would never vanish. But after being involved in the game at the college level for six years, I now understand that the love for the game does die down for a majority of college student-athletes. Whether it be because of the high demands of being a student-athlete, injuries, the time commitment or other factors, the majority DO NOT finish their playing careers.

My signing class in 2011 to Humboldt had 50% of the signees complete their eligibility at Humboldt State, by far the LARGEST number at the school in the past 6+ years. There were times in my career where I thought about quitting or transferring because of injuries, playing on a 0-11 team, or having a desire to play at a higher level. Despite all of the adversity, I'm forever grateful that I stuck it out and did what so many other of my teammates weren't able to do. I fell in love with the school that I attended and the town that it resided in so much so that I spent four summers back at school instead of going home and I even came back to coach.

To give an idea of how low the retention of college football players is, Humboldt State had 3 players who signed as

Seniors in High School and finished their careers at Humboldt State in 2014 (13%), 12 players in 2015 (50%), 3 in 2016 (13%) and are projected to have another 3 in 2017 (13%). Oregon State University had 5 student-athletes from their 2012 signing class complete their eligibility (20%). Completing a college football career where a student-athlete begins their career is UNCOMMON and this needs to be taken into consideration before making a decision as to which school you will attend.

A, B, & C Lists of Schools

Develop lists of schools that you would like to pursue, creating tiers of A, B, & C groups. Your "A List" schools will be your dream school(s). Your "B List" will be comprised of schools that are likely your best fit and most likely to be admitted and play football. Your "C List" might be comprised of schools that are closer to home, some that you may be willing to travel long distances to if it means continuing to play football or even ones you would attend if you don't play football.

Take the example of one high school junior who started his C list with a number of Division III schools and an in-state University (no football). If all his other schools fell through, he would decide between playing football and simply being a college student at a large Pac-12 university. His B List schools were a number of Division II and NAIA schools. Lastly, his A list schools were a number of FCS schools that offered the potential of a preferred walk-on offer.

His A list was a reach, his B list was more in line with his FIT, but his C list provided a backstop if football was no longer part of the equation or if all his B list options didn't work out.

The Resume of Your Life
What Picture Does it Paint?

8

People are complex beings with many different roles that they function in daily. Over the course of a day, you can function in the role of child, sibling, student, athlete, captain, teammate, employee, volunteer, tutor, and friend. No one role will fully reveal who you are, but each taken together can begin to paint a picture of the person you are.

High School Transcript

Most college coaches will ask for a prospective student-athlete's academic transcript early in the recruiting or evaluation process. This single document will present the first picture of who you are as a person. The first thing it will tell the coaches is whether or not you have the likelihood of qualifying academically for admission and competition. If you aren't likely to qualify, most coaches will move on as they can't waste time on players that will never play for them.

Your resume can show coaches what type of student and how hard of a worker you are. It can show that you are someone who challenges themselves with difficult classes. It could demonstrate that you are someone who has worked through adversity, like some early academic struggles or some type of family/personal crisis.

Lastly, your transcript can demonstrate to a coach that you are capable of excelling in multiple arenas. That you are capable of balancing all of the demands that are placed on today's college student-athletes. Taking control and focusing on your academics in high school is a critical step in your future success.

Volunteerism, Clubs and Other Activities

Are you involved in other activities besides just football? Are you involved in drama, music, school clubs, or other types of non-athletic activities? Do you give back to your school, your community, your family? Do you have part-time work? Smart coaches are looking for dynamic people that aren't already burned out on football and that will contribute to the vitality of their team and the college campus. Give thought to making yourself a better person by thinking of others first, serving others and by broadening your interests and friends in things besides just football.

Evaluation Period

Beginning in the spring of an athlete's junior year of high school, college coaches may visit on campus for the purpose of evaluating prospective student-athletes (April 15 to May 30). This process can include getting an unofficial transcript, talking with coaches, teachers, and administrators, as well as watching athletes work out, practice, or compete in spring sports. This 45 day "evaluation period" is critical to most college programs' recruiting. Coaches want to learn as much information about the character, work-ethic, academic achievement, and athletic prowess of prospects. Talking face to face with coaches, administrators, and teachers is a powerful means of assessing future players.

What will your teachers and administrators say about you? Do you cause problems in school? Are you a leader? Understand that before a school is going to commit thousands of dollars on a student-athlete, they are going to do their due diligence to help them understand the type of person they are committing to and investing in ("hiring").

Strive to live a life worthy of being examined. Because that is what's going to happen to any prospective college athlete.

Social Media Presence

One of the first things that coaches will do in the early stages of evaluating and recruiting a high school athlete is to look them up and connect with them on social media. NCAA rules permit coaches to message athletes over Facebook and Twitter without restriction, even before they can mail letters or call on the phone. When a high school athlete is "followed" by a college coach, this is a big deal to their social status and their ego. It is part of the "recruiting process" and how coaches look to build connections with high school prospects.

If a college coach does follow you on Twitter, the most commonly used social media site for recruiting, you should follow them back. Next take the time to send them a personal message. Once you follow each other, it enables you to send a Direct Message, do it! Make sure before you send the message that you do some homework on the school and coach. Do not send a generic message asking for the coach to watch your film or for a scholarship. Separate yourself from others in this part of the process!

When a coach does follow you, the first thing they are going to do is to look at the student-athlete's social media page. What type of things do they post? What things do they favorite or like? Are there inappropriate, off-color, insensitive, or vulgar posts? These things can raise significant red flags for coaches or schools.

Once a student-athlete commits to attend or has signed a letter of intent with a college, many schools will issue a welcome letter that warns them about their social media presence. I remember our son receiving a letter from Oregon State in the spring of his senior year, shortly after signing day. It was personally signed by the head coach and it specifically addressed his use of social media. He was told, more or less, that if he wouldn't feel good about his mom reading every post, then he shouldn't post it; if his account is offensive, then it would be best to delete it. Once on campus, he would be held accountable for being a good representative of the University and those who can't uphold this standard can be dismissed from the team and the school.

Remember, colleges are trying to get a picture into who you are as a person. Are you someone that they can trust to work hard, stay out of trouble and be a good teammate during your time at school? Does your track record demonstrate someone who can juggle all the demands of being a student and an athlete? As they investigate your life, what is the image that they are going to see? Your high school transcripts, your social media presence… talking to your football coaches; talking to your high school principal, counselors, lunchroom workers, teachers, other sports coaches. All of these small images, woven together, begin to paint a picture of who you are.

Your character is revealed by the things you do when no one is looking over your shoulder. Examine yourself. Google your name. What are the first things that are going to pop up when a coach does this basic task? It is never too late to make a change. Start to become the person you want to be. Make choices that are aligned with the direction you want your life to go.

Don't make a $100,000 Mistake
By Taylor Mitchell

In my first role as a College Football coach at Harding University, social media was the first thing we as coaches checked on as a part of our background check on potential student-athletes. Yes, it may be unfair to judge a young kid that you've never met before based off of his "Tweets", but when a University is looking to invest their money, thousands of dollars, into a complete stranger, questions must be answered through proper research and due diligence. Since Harding was a private Christian school, it was easy for the coaches to get an idea if a potential recruit was going to be a good fit and be able to abide by the school's rules.

While there are negatives to social media, I have found as a coach that it makes connecting, discovering and communicating with potential recruits extremely easy. Social media is a great way for coaches to share content for marketing purposes that recruits can easily see. This allows recruits to get a rare glimpse and look into the program that they may have never considered or visited before. I receive dozens of notifications every day between getting new followers and direct messages. This allows me to easily go through and find new recruits, especially if they HAVE THEIR FILM PINNED TO THEIR PROFILE/IN THEIR BIO. If a kids profile turned out clean and had good film, I would typically follow them and then message them to begin a conversation

Whenever a kid receives an offer, you can typically expect for them to post on social media that they have been offered by school XYZ. As a coach, it definitely makes you question whether the potential recruit has an interest in playing at the next level or if he simply enjoys the attention of being recruited. University of Washington Head Football Coach Chris Petersen was recently discussing the recruiting process and the difficulty it presents in making sure that they land the right kind of kids. He stated that they have to ask themselves, "Is he really our kind of guy? Does he truly love football? On a scale of 1-10, does he love it at a 15? I make a big thing about that nowadays, because I think so many kids don't love football. They love recruiting. They love being recruited. But when it comes down to loving the game when it's Week 8, you're sore and tired and you're going to go out to practice to get better. Those guys are hard to find." If a kid truly does love football and is posting about receiving offers, it is going to catch the eyes of coaches. If a rival or neighboring school is talking to a player, other schools are going to take notice and take a look at the potential recruit and consider offering them as well.

Social media can be a very positive tool to assist a student-athlete and their recruiting process, if it is utilized responsibly and effectively.

Developing a Marketing Plan

Research, Goal Setting & Pursuit of Them

9

If you have an idea of the level of play and types of schools that you are going to pursue, then you are ready to start researching schools. Spend time on school websites looking at the majors offered, number of students, breakdown of the student body, student/professor ratios, traditions, photos of the campus, special events, etc. Talk to alumni or students from your high school or area that attend these schools. Visit schools during your spring break or summer vacations (get a campus tour before/after every camp or game you attend on a college campus. Admission offices will typically offer campus tours year-round). Bear in mind that summertime visits don't present a realistic picture of a college campus when it is full of students, but it will give you an idea of what the campus and local area are like.

Develop target list of schools creating A, B, and C lists of schools. The "A List" schools are your reach schools (academically, financially, and athletically). The "B List" schools are in your zone, but still might be a reach in one or more areas (academics, financial, or athletics). The "C List" would be schools that are closer to home, more affordable, or options if you don't play athletics in college.

Creating a Highlight Film

While you are researching schools, you will want to create a highlight film of your VARSITY football season. Here are a few tips and reminders as you are creating your highlight film.

Depending on the level of play and what year you are in school, the highlight film can be a work in progress. Some schools that are evaluating you will ask for your first three or four games of your junior or senior year. Be sure to give your film an appropriate title so coaches can easily locate the film they are looking for, there is no need to put a cute/inappropriate title. Players should go back weekly and flag their best plays from that week's game for the eventual final highlight tape.

First, put your name, jersey #, positions played, cell phone number, and Twitter handle on the front of the video. You can also add your stats and major accolades that you may have received as well. Most players produce their film through the HUDL software and this information gets posted at the beginning of the video. Next, remember to keep it simple and clean. You aren't submitting a film to the Academy for consideration of an award. Trim plays down to the essential elements that a coach will want to see. For example, if you are an offensive lineman, the coach doesn't need to see your running back going 80 yards for the touchdown. Show your block and your "finish", then move on. Coaches like to see players "finish" plays, playing to the whistle, pursuing a tackle or a player continuing to block to the very end of the play. There's no need for music, but if you feel you must do it, make sure it is clean and something that could be played for 2nd graders or your mom.

Highlight yourself at *the beginning of plays*, especially if you move around a lot, like an offensive lineman that flips back and forth between left & right tackle or a defensive back that plays corner, safety and nickel. Highlighting yourself in the middle of a play can make the video look spotty and can take away from your big play, do it pre-snap! Be sure to show a variety of plays at the beginning of your highlight tape as well. Coaches don't want to see a WR only catching vertical routes or an OL pass setting or down blocking play after play, make sure there is a diverse assortment of plays!

Keep the film to around 5 minutes with your BEST plays in the very beginning. Anything longer is too much and will rarely be watched. Most coaches can see what they like or don't like in the first 60 seconds. Former University of Nebraska Director of Player Personnel Ryan Gunderson said to, "Always put your best stuff first. Don't save your best stuff for last. Put it up front. You may only get 30 seconds or a minute of somebody's time and if that doesn't impress them right away, they're not going to turn your film back on."

MOST IMPORTANT - Have your position coach review your film before you begin to share it. I've seen players post a "highlight" as their first play not realizing that it actually makes them look bad.

Questionnaires

Next, you will want to visit to the school websites and fill out the athletic recruiting questionnaire. These are typically located on the individual sport's webpage and may also be called the "recruiting questionnaire". If interested, you can also fill out the university's general student information request form to get more information on the school. Completing the recruiting questionnaire will let the football program know you are interested and it will get your contact information into their database. This makes it easier for them to communicate with you if and when they deem you a "recruit".

The Questionnaire will ask for all of your contact information, cell phone, email, social media addresses (Facebook, Twitter, Instagram). It will ask about your grade point, test scores, outside activities, and other sports you play. It will likely ask about your physical traits, height, weight, 40 time, vertical jump, and strength. Most importantly it will ask for the web address of your highlight film and your coach's contact information.

Camps & Showcases

There are lots of private groups and recruiting services that host "showcase" camps, 7 on 7 tournaments and "combines" making the claim that they will be able to help promote, get exposure or get your athlete recruited. In some sports like soccer, volleyball and basketball, college coaches will attend "showcase" tournaments to evaluate prospects, but this is not allowed with football. Per NCAA rules, college coaches cannot attend "showcase" events or 7 on 7 tournaments in which they are not coaching or hosting the event. The rules do not allow them to even watch video from these events. That doesn't mean that attending one of these camps can't be worthwhile, but with limited time and financial resources, it is best to be strategic in which events you attend. It is important to also recognize that your body only has so many "bullets" in it, so it is wise not to waste them on unnecessary activities.

NCAA rules allow college coaches to work at summer camps in the months of June and July for a period of 15 consecutive days. Most schools will host their own camps with several purposes in mind. The first is to teach the game of football to youth and high school players. Second is to provide their young assistant coaches with an opportunity to get coaching experience. Next is to utilize the school's facilities to create excitement and to show them off to the community. Lastly and most importantly, schools host these camps as a way to evaluate prospects and recruit players.

"Rising Star" or "Elite" type camps hosted by colleges are the best means for players to get directly evaluated by college coaches and for college coaches to evaluate and recruit players. Coaches can work out, instruct, and evaluate a prospect with their own eyes. Many coaches will specifically invite a prospect to attend their camp, just so they can evaluate them in person. This helps them to determine whether an athlete is someone they would like to recruit. Additionally, coaches will invite players that are already committed to their school or that they have offered and are actively recruiting. This allows them personal contact with the prospect that normally isn't permissible until fall of the prospect's senior year (there are exceptions if a recruit phones a coach or visits campus). This allows them the chance to start building a relationship with the recruit and their family.

Additionally, smaller schools will often invite higher level schools in their area to attend or to help out at their camps which are one form of a "satellite camp." These larger schools that come in typically have recruiting ties in the particular areas where they help run camps. A DIII school may invite DI-FBS, DI-FCS, and DII coaches since they will all be recruiting different levels of athletes. Higher tier programs know that the majority of players attending the camp will not be a fit for them, but they will be able to spend time working out the few that are. This creates opportunities for more kids to find a good fit and it helps coaches at lower level schools with fewer recruiting resources to have a large number of kids on their campus. A camp that will have multiple schools from multiple levels of play is the ideal camp opportunity.

A few things to know about these camps. First, most schools tend to price these camps less expensively than for-profit camps. They don't want price to deter attendance and the college program isn't concerned about making a profit. Their only concern is identifying prospects and getting a chance to recruit them in person. Sometimes when an athlete is being recruited by multiple schools, they will try to attend a number of camps in a very short period of time. Coaches will make accommodations for players that they are recruiting. This could be letting the player attend the camp for a shorter amount of time than the full length of the camp, because they have to leave early or arrive late. This could be working a player out before or after the normal camp hours.

Many college programs or coaches have started affiliating with independent groups who host regional camps in large metropolitan areas which is another form of satellite camps. College coaches may coach at the camp, work out players, evaluate, and recruit just like they do at their own camps provided the camp meets a few requirements. These include being an "open" camp (not an invite only) and the price is the same for all attendees. These satellite camps provide a less expensive alternative for athletes versus paying travel costs to reach an out of state school. These camps are another way for athletes to catch a coach's eye for the first time or to make a personal connection with a coach, especially if you are already being recruited. These camps can start to morph into "meat markets" with so many attendees that only a few very elite athletes are given much time and attention.

Team Camps

Team camps are an important component of many high school programs' summer routine and off-season program. Colleges host "team" camps to make money. They are typically very crowded with 500 to 1,000 players attending depending on the school that is hosting the camp. The high school teams' coaches attend with their players and coach them throughout the majority of the camp. The college coaches lead some drills and components of the camp, but the high school coaches are still heavily involved. College coaches still have the opportunity to take advantage of having access to any commits or prospects at this camp. Team camps are best viewed as benefitting team chemistry and team development for your upcoming season. College coaches WILL be watching every drill and scrimmage so you CAN get noticed at these camps.

If your team is attending a team camp, it is still recommended that you go and participate with your teammates. One way to get noticed as a player is by winning football games and summertime is a great time to begin building team chemistry.

Obviously if there are other schools recruiting you and if they are serious about you being a potential player for their program, most high school coaches will help you out however they can by letting you attend these other camps.

Wear and Tear

Another consideration in attending camps is to recognize the amount of wear and tear that you are subjecting your body. For this reason, it is important to be strategic in how many and which camps you attend. The most important thing you can do to help your collegiate future is to have a good HIGH SCHOOL season. The worst thing you could do is to wear yourself out and play your season with a nagging injury because you "over-camped" in the summer. Even worse would be for you to arrive at your "A List" school's camp and perform poorly due to exhaustion or injury from over camping.

"Elite" Camps

There are lots of elite non-padded camps, combines and All-Star games that offer an allure of celebrity, elite level competition, potential promotion and discovery. No camp in and of itself is inherently bad. It is doing too many of them that is the problem. Parents are wise to guide their children through this maze and to help to prevent their child from being exploited. Elite camps like "The Opening" and "The Elite 11" are prestigious, televised and certainly provide a great amount of exposure for athletes. But if your son is already being actively recruited or is already committed, more "exposure" or higher rankings will mean NOTHING. An injury at an elite camp when you have already accepted a scholarship offer doesn't seem like a great use of your time or your "bullets".

Non-padded camps and combines aren't something that college coaches give much consideration to in the first place. They trust their eyes and their evaluation of varsity game film. Remember, there are no 7 on 7 teams or two-hand touch games in college. Non-padded camps or 7 on 7 tournaments are not REAL FOOTBALL. Stanford isn't going to throw the ball 4 times from the 2 yard line on first and goal! Don't put too much weight in non-padded football activities.

Specialist Camps

For kickers, punters and long snappers, there are a few organizations who focus on training just these "specialists". These groups do an excellent job of teaching the fundamentals for each position. Each will proclaim themselves to be THE expert for their field and THE go to person if your son wants to play in college. They provide "rankings" and detailed evaluations of players that include actual stats like hang times, snap times, distances, 40 yard dash times, and the like.

These groups can get carried away with constant self-promotion, encouraging athletes to attend every event they hold. Some families get caught up in this hype machine and will spend the equivalent of a year's worth of college costs on travel and camp fees. Parents and athletes can get lured into "competing" for better rankings and will keep attending more camps, when they are no longer necessary.

Attending one or two of these specialist camps is typically adequate for purposes of being evaluated. Going to a large group camp for the specific purpose of improving your skills is not the best use of your money. It would be better spent on small group or one on one lessons if you are wanting to get coached up on your skills.

NOTE: Lower level schools with limited support staffs and recruiting budgets will utilize the ranking lists to identify potential specialists. Smaller programs will sift through ranking lists to identify specialists that fit their program. The highest rank isn't necessarily the criteria they are looking at. They will look at prospects' physical characteristics, athletic abilities, academics, and their proximity to campus. Ideally, schools want to utilize a limited number of roster spots on specialists and see them use up their full eligibility with their school (a good fit). Being on the list is more important than being the top player on the list. If you have dollars to spend on training, use them for private lessons, not on travel and expensive camp fees.

Larger programs will try to have specialists attend their elite or "rising stars" camps. Some schools will bring in the aforementioned specialist training groups to run a specialists only camp. It is critical for specialists to focus on attending camps at schools that are looking to recruit someone in your class, as schools will host summer camps EVERY year, regardless of whether they are looking to sign someone in your class.

Conclusion – Summer Camps

Summer Football camps represent the BEST opportunity for athletes to connect, work out for, or get on the radar with college coaches. **Therefore, it is important for players to wisely target the camps that they attend.** If a player already has colleges offering scholarships, there is no need to attend 8 camps to show "everyone" how good of an athlete you are. You may not need to attend ANY camps. BE SMART! Don't get caught up in the Summer Camp Circus. If you already have scholarship offers, but there is a school that you are really interested in attending and the coaches want to evaluate you, then attend this camp. If you want to see what it is like interacting with the coaches at one of your top schools, then attend this camp. If you have several schools that seem interested in you, then attend these camps.

The Recruiting "Waterfall"

Timing of Recruiting Varies by Level

11

Imagine that you are a college recruiting coordinator. You have 50,000 high school seniors to sort through and identify as prospects that will be a good fit for your school and level of play. You don't want to waste time pursuing athletes that are "too good" for your program, yet you always want to get the very best athletes available.

Now imagine that every high school and junior college athlete are like fish being dumped into a large lake. A river flows out of the lake and drops over a series of waterfalls into a number of large pools where fishermen (coaches) are waiting to catch their "lunkers". Some fisherman are located in the top pools and they will quickly "fish out" their limit (25 athletes) and call it a recruiting season. All the other fisherman in the pool fill their limit and the remaining fish go over the falls into the next pool. Fisherman wait there to see what players will fall to their pool. And this continues on down the line until every school at every level has filled their limit.

The "recruiting" process timing can vary widely depending on the level of play, caliber of athlete, and prestige of the program. The very best athletes are targeted in the spring of their sophomore year by the top programs (Alabama, USC, Ohio State, Michigan) – i.e. the "Top Pool". The remaining athletes go over the waterfall and into the next pool. It is here that the next tier of athletes are recruited by Power 5 programs (ACC, Big 10, Big 12, Pac-12 and SEC) early in their junior year. The remaining athletes go over the falls to the next pool where lower level DI-FBS schools will target athletes in the spring of their junior year. The remaining athletes drop over the falls into the next pool, where DI-FCS will begin to recruit players in the spring of their junior year and fall of their senior year.

FCS schools like to wait until later in the recruiting cycle to pursue athletes. They know many athletes will choose a DI-FBS school over a DI-FCS program because of the perception of FBS football being a "higher level" (though practically and competitively, that may not be the case). FCS schools have limited coaching staffs and recruiting budgets, so maximizing their use is essential. There are cases where they will target a known player in late spring of their junior year. This could be a local high school star or someone that has previously attended their summer camps. Typically, DI-FCS schools will offer players later in the fall of their senior year, sometimes as late as January just before signing day. Some FCS schools will offer players the night before signing day or days after signing day when scholarships are turned down by other athletes. Additionally, FCS schools will offer "preferred walk-ons" to players once they are out of scholarship roster spots.

Many people fail to recognize that National Letter of Intent "Signing Day" is merely the FIRST day of the signing period that runs through the first of April.

DII Schools experience a similar phenomenon to the FCS schools. Coaches may offer known players in the summer before their senior year or early in the fall, but their typical recruiting cycle is to spend the fall evaluating players. Their recruits are high school seniors and sophomores at junior colleges, comprising their prospect list. Their coaching and recruiting resources are much smaller than FCS schools, so they have to be extremely judicious in their use. Many DII schools' first step will be to invite players on an unofficial visit, to come watch a game and meet the coaches. A next step will be to offer players an official visit, most often in January. It is on these official visits or soon thereafter, that players are "offered" a scholarship and told exactly how much (in dollars) it is. It is VERY

COMMON, for DII schools to continue to recruit players AFTER "Signing Day". This is because the window for football players to sign their National Letter of Intent runs all the way through the first of April. Many people believe that "Signing Day" (the first Wednesday in February) is on one day, but it runs for almost two months. DII schools use the full extent of this window to fill their recruiting classes. Very often DII schools will be recruiting athletes that have been offered preferred walk-ons at DI-FCS schools.

The recruiting process is very fluid and it works similar to a NFL draft board. The recruiting coordinator at colleges typically will develop recruiting boards with recruits ranked by position group. As their top players commit to higher level or other comparable schools, they will continue to work down their list to the next best player. This is why "tweener" type players can get offered a scholarship or a preferred walk-on late in the process by DI-FCS schools, while DII programs have been actively recruiting said player.

Division III schools typically "recruit" players much later in the process. They will provide unofficial visits that involve an overnight stay, attendance to a sporting event, visiting with players on the team and a comprehensive review of the campus. DIII schools can provide a paid visit to prospective students if this is a normal part of their school's regular student recruiting process. There is no "signing date" for DIII schools, so they recruit all throughout the spring even into summer. The first hurdle for every DIII prospect is gaining admission to the school. With this accomplished, the next hurdle is the financial aid award process. Students need to have completed the FAFSA along with providing any financial information requested by the school. You can expect to hear back from schools anywhere from mid-March to early April. Schools will provide a "financial award" letter that details their financial aid package. These typically consist of scholarships, subsidized loans, private student loans, work study, and a family EFC (expected family contribution).

It is a good idea for student-athletes considering DIII schools for athletics to apply to multiple schools. The reason is that the range of financial aid can vary widely from school to school and this allows them the opportunity to find the best fit of academics and athletics in line with their budget. One college may offer $20,000 in financial aid that consists of just student loans and a family EFC of $10,000. While another school may provide $15,000 in scholarships and work study, $5,000 in loans and $10,000 in EFC for mom and dad. Both schools cost $30,000, both schools provided $20,000 in "financial aid", but one is a substantially better deal. Cost will play a critical part in your school choice, so it is a good idea to try to give yourself a range of options.

Athletic Scholarship

Financial Aid Considerations

12

DI-FBS Schools can only offer full scholarships to a total of 85 players. A "scholarship offer" by a DI-FBS football will be for the full cost of attendance, tuition & fees, room & board, and books. In almost all cases, this scholarship will include summer school, as student-athletes have to be enrolled in summer classes in order to stay on campus, work-out with strength coaches and receive their monthly stipend checks (for off-campus housing and meals). Larger schools in the Power 5 (ACC, Big 10, Big 12, Pac 12 & SEC) also include an additional amount in their monthly stipends to cover the "full cost of attendance". This is meant to offset costs like travel to and from campus, parking passes, clothing, and personal entertainment, since they aren't able to hold down jobs or work summer internships due to their athletic commitments.

DI-FBS Student-athletes that live off-campus receive a "stipend" check to cover housing and meals. The amount of this stipend can vary during off-season and in-season when the team is providing a "training table" (a dining hall or meals when the team travels). Having these meals provided reduces the amount of the stipend. The cost of attendance is determined by Federal Cost of Attendance figures that are based on the specific average costs of housing in each college town.

DI-FCS, DII and NAIA schools can offer full or partial scholarships. These schools are limited in their numbers of scholarships by their association (NCAA or NAIA), by their conference, and by their school's financial budget.

For example, the NCAA sets the maximum number of athletic scholarship equivalents at 36 for DII football programs. But a conference can establish a LOWER scholarship maximum for all the members of their conference, say 30. Lastly, each school can establish a lower number of scholarships for their sports teams based on their financial budget. The conference may establish football maximum scholarships at 25 for all the members, but individual schools may only be able to provide 15 or 20 scholarships to their football coach.

What exactly is being "offered" by a partial scholarship school can vary widely by conference, school, your position played, and by how in-demand the student-athlete is. Some schools "offer" literally HUNDREDS of athletes, but they provide no details of what the offer is. It is not uncommon for DII schools to tell a player that they are "recruiting" said athlete. The next step may be for the school to offer the athlete an "official visit". This is a one-time school paid recruiting visit to the campus that may include some or all of the transportation costs, hotel, meals, and attendance to other campus sporting events. While on campus, the school may reveal the details of the "offer" or they may tell the athlete that they'll have more details in the days following the visit.

Division III schools, California Junior Colleges, Ivy & Pioneer League schools do not offer athletic scholarships. An "offer" from these schools is merely a formal way of telling a player, "we want you to play for us." Because there are no scholarship dollars provided, there are typically no roster limits. Think of these teams like an elite high school team. If you are in school here, you may come out for football. But after you are on the team, competition will rule the day. Regardless of whether you are at Harvard, MIT, or the University of San Diego, the best players will play. Applying for admission to these schools will result in a notification of acceptance and an eventual offer of financial aid. Some schools provide some

"Institutional Grant" dollars to their football coaches that effectively function as an athletic scholarship.

Note: Some Division III schools provide financial incentives to their coaches for maintaining minimum roster sizes. It is not uncommon for some DIII programs to have up to 150 players on the roster. Higher education is a big business, just like Division I athletics. Don't be duped. It is basic commerce and negotiation of price and services. The student-athlete is looking for the best fit for them, which is typically the highest level of play where they will see the field and excel. The coach is looking for the best players to fill a roster who will win games. The college or university wants the maximum exposure for their school along with the maximum revenues and greatest effectiveness at educating as many students as they can. In an ideal negotiation of terms, everyone wins in some areas and gives in others. This book is about providing you with as much insight and wisdom to aid you in your "recruiting journey".

Nuances & Insights

On Levels of Play & Position Groups

13
Division I-FBS

This is BIG TIME football. It is a business, period. More money, more scrutiny, more pressure, less balance. Big promises, big possibilities, big challenges. The benefits are BIG: first class facilities, great levels of support (academics, career, athletic training, nutritionists, strength & conditioning), comfortable travel accommodations, plenty of food, and first class uniforms/equipment. The downsides are just as big: high pressure, high demands, little down time, extreme competitiveness for playing time, and coaching turnover.

The best guys will play. Playing time decisions are all about business. It isn't personal and players shouldn't take it personal.

Players should only expect to get 3 or 4 extended breaks away from school each year: spring break, a week early in summers after the end of the spring quarter/semester, maybe the week before fall camp starts later in July/early August and sometime during the Holidays. Players will not be home for Thanksgiving (as this is typically the last game of the regular season). If a team makes it to a marquee bowl game played around New Year's Day, then players may not get a chance to come home for Christmas.

Players can expect to arrive on campus early in the summer of their freshman year and to spend every summer on campus taking summer classes and training intensely for the upcoming season.

Generally speaking at FBS schools, if players are living up their end of the deal, they can expect their scholarship to be renewed each year. This means working hard, being on time, going to class, having a good attitude, and staying out of trouble.

Division I-FCS

Though a step below FBS football, the top FCS schools can and do compete on par with many FBS programs. In general, FCS schools will vary from their FBS counterparts mostly in the depth of support staff and their overall operating budget. Some may or may not require summer school attendance once you are in school. Many players will stay in the area to train, but they may get summer jobs, unlike their FBS counterparts.

Preferred walk-ons are a critical component of how FCS schools build their rosters. They tend to have more roster movement than a FBS school. This is due specifically to the limit of 63 scholarships and 95 max roster at the start of fall camp. Consider that most FCS schools will only travel 55 or fewer players to an away game (this number is limited by their conference rules – each conference sets a limit). FBS schools in the Pac-12 can travel 75 players (with 85 on scholarship). If a player is on scholarship at a FCS school, the coaches have an expectation that the player will contribute early in their career.

At the levels of play where partial scholarships are provided (DI-FCS, DII, and NAIA), rosters are managed much more proactively. Sometimes players will arrive on campus and the coaches will realize that they player is either not as good as they thought or they just aren't developing after a couple seasons. When this happens, players can have their scholarship reduced, be taken completely off scholarship or be released from the team. Top programs with an expectation to win and perform, tend to be much more active in turning their rosters over. It's a business.

As players progress in a FCS program and they move up the depth chart, they can often expect their scholarship dollars to increase. There are LOTS of variables in play when it comes to managing scholarships and a team roster, but this is a general rule with lots of exceptions.

Division II

Represents a "more balanced" athletic experience. In summer, athletes typically go home for periods of time, travel back & forth, or get a summer job near campus. Student-Athletes can also pursue summer internships (perhaps shorter in length than a normal internship). It is against NCAA rules for Division II coaches to mandate/require their athletes to stay for summer workouts, but there can be huge advantages to staying. Participation in student government, intramural athletics or other campus clubs are possible. Competing in two sports happens.

DII Athletes are permitted to transfer to another DII school one time in their career without having to sit out a year. DII schools will get lots of junior college transfers, as well as DI "drop down" athletes. Expect intense competition like all other levels.

Division III

There are no "athletic" scholarships provided by Division III schools. The majority of DIII schools are private institutions that are traditionally much more expensive than public schools. They are also typically more difficult to get admitted into. Many schools will provide significant academic scholarships for students with good grades and strong test scores. Very often, these scholarships will make the cost of attendance more comparable to a public university. Additionally, some schools provide their coaches with discretionary "institutional grants" that they can use to entice top recruits in their financial aid package. Effectively, these are "athletic" scholarships.

A positive at the DIII level is that some programs will field a JV team that will play games against other JV teams.

Specialists

DI-FBS programs will typically only dedicate 1 scholarship to each of a punter, a kicker and a long snapper (3 total). Back-ups are most often walk-ons. Sometimes the next recruit will come on as a walk-on while the veteran plays out his eligibility. If the walk-on has impressed, then they can assume the scholarship of the departing player. If they've shown inconsistency in practice, expect other walk-ons to show up to compete for the roster sport. If another recruit is brought in on scholarship after a walk-on has been waiting for the position, this is effectively notice that the other player is in line to take the job. The walk-on may be invited to stay on the roster, but it will continue to be without a scholarship.

College coaches can get in a pinch and call on the "specialist" training groups to find out who they view as the best long snappers or punters that are still available. But ultimately, every college football coach is going to offer a scholarship or roster spot based on THEIR evaluation.

Besides honing their skills, specialists should focus on identifying the level of play that they likely FIT. Next they should identify schools that will likely be looking to take a specialist in their class. This will aid them in developing their marketing plan and the schools they will target.

Quarterbacks

Quarterbacks are likely the most challenging position group on a football team. In the majority of instances, only one quarterback will play in games. Programs will typically recruit in one scholarship QB a year. DI-FBS schools will try to have at least 4 scholarship QBs on the roster. It is not uncommon for top programs to have 8 or more QBs on the roster, the lot of them being walk-ons. Programs will typically divide QB practice reps like this: the #1 will get 8 out of every 10 reps with the #2 will get 2 out of the 10. The #3 will occasionally get 1 of the 10 reps, but the majority of the time they are watching. The #4 and 5 QBs will typically serve as scout team QBs. If one is more athletic than the other, they may take the majority of the reps on weeks when the team is facing a dual threat QB.

Quarterbacks who show up on campus as development projects will often find that there is very little time for their coaches to "develop" them. The majority of practice time is focused on game prep and winning. Development projects often end up switching positions. Athletic QBs make good safeties, wide receivers, or outside linebackers.

Quarterbacks need to analyze the depth charts of the teams that are recruiting them. A QB that starts as a freshman (that is performing adequately) may likely own the starting spot for another 2 or 3 years. A team that has a roster weighted with upper classmen will typically look for a JuCo or graduate transfer to provide a ready to play option to compete for the job. Additionally, they may sign multiple QBs in one class to help to replenish their roster.

Junior colleges can provide young quarterbacks with an ideal environment to develop. Players that took up the position late in high school may want to find a place where they can play immediately. Playing at a JuCo can help to continue a player's development, especially compared to sitting on the bench or standing around at a higher level of play. Additionally, Junior Colleges have a slightly different tack on player development than four year programs. JuCo coaches are focused on player development and placement into four year schools, whereas four year schools are focused on WINNING.

Finding the best fit in terms of level of play, competition, and academic environment is the ultimate goal for every player, including quarterbacks. The majority of QBs will never see the field at their first school out of high school. Many QBs will transfer schools to find a better fit, switch positions, or stop playing. Quarterbacks should expect to be low on the depth chart when they arrive on campus, to have to work hard, and to wait their turn to move up the depth chart.

Walk-ons

The life of a walk-on is one of the most challenging for any student-athlete. From the very beginning, the cards are stacked against you. You are expected to be as committed as every scholarship athlete without the school being committed to you. In many instances, walk-ons are going to great personal expense for the opportunity of just being on the team.

Remember this general rule: If a team is unwilling to offer you scholarship dollars, they are telling you that you are low on their priority list or depth chart.

At full scholarship DI-FBS schools, the majority of the time no scholarship means no playing time. At partial scholarship programs, walking-on is a normal part of the process of working your way up the depth chart. As you move up, you will likely earn scholarship dollars.

Most walk-ons are expected to serve as scout team players and nothing more. Every team needs bodies for the starters to go against in practice while they are installing each week's game plan. Selflessness and a team first attitude is required as a walk-on.

Every year, there will be athletes recruited as a walk-on under special circumstances. Examples are a player who suffered a major injury with uncertainty as to their ability to recover; a player who missed their senior year; a player who just started playing the game or who switched positions late in their career; specialists who will be waiting to compete for a starting spot once the starter graduates; a player who played football in a small school conference or against extremely weak competition. All of these athletes can be recruited as a walk-on with the idea that they could earn a scholarship.

When you are offered as a "walk-on", it is up to you to ask for clarity about your role. Remember, coaches may promise things, but it is up to you to be rational about your ability and your opportunity. Is this the only DI-FBS school to offer you a preferred walk-on position? Did you have any DI-FCS scholarship offers? Or was it just DII scholarship offers? Are their special circumstances to your walk-on offer? Taking all of these into account can help you make an informed decision.

Transferring

Part of growing up is recognizing that not everything is going to be perfect. And sometimes circumstances will dictate that a change should happen. Coaches make promises that aren't realistic; coaches get fired or leave to take another job; you aren't meshing with your position coach or with the team; other players arrive that make playing time a longshot; you realize that you are outmatched; the campus/academic setting is not a good fit; as a specialist, you lose out to another player. Events like these play out every year on every team. OK, you realize the fit is bad, but how do you proceed?

The first step to transferring is talking to your coach and then the athletic department. You will be requesting "Permission to Contact" other schools. Your athletic department has to issue a letter granting you permission and you will have to show this letter before other schools will talk with you. If your current school does not grant you permission to contact, then no other NCAA programs will be able to offer you an athletic scholarship for a period of one year.

If you are on athletic scholarship, this means you signed a National Letter of Intent (NLI), which is a legally binding contract for a period of one year. You will eventually have to request your Release from your NLI. There are many nuances and rules established by the NCAA and conferences around transfers (see Transfer Chapter), so it is important to make sure you understand the implications of changing schools. These vary based on your academic standing, if you qualified academically when you entered college and other factors. These rules vary by the level of play (DI-FBS, FCS, DII, & DIII) and by the association if you are transferring to and from (NCAA to NAIA, or NCAA to JuCo).

Here is a suggestion based on our family's firsthand experience with a DI transfer. If you are a scholarship athlete looking to transfer, ask just for permission to contact other schools, not to withdraw from school or seek your release from your NLI. Depending on the time of year, it might be difficult time to connect with coaches and find a spot to transfer to in a hurry. Therefore, it would be wise to continue taking classes, stay on scholarship, and keep receiving your stipend checks. Once you identify a program or programs that are interested in offering you a scholarship, then you can get released from your NLI.

Junior College

Attending a Junior College can be a great way for a young person to mature emotionally, grow academically, and develop athletically. Junior colleges are the only option for student-athletes who don't qualify academically to compete at the NCAA level right out of high school.

Junior college coaches are accustomed to working with both raw and college ready athletes to prepare them to move on to compete at four year schools. For a raw, inexperienced athlete, the junior college level represents an ideal place to continue to learn and develop. Redshirting is allowed at junior colleges, so many players will spend three years at a junior college before moving on to a 4 year school for their final two years of eligibility.

For an academic qualifier (someone who meets the NCAA eligibility requirements) who chooses to attend a junior college, they are not required to obtain an associate's degree before they move on to a four year school. It is possible that they could play for one year and move on the next year to a 4 year school. Non-qualifiers must graduate with their associate's degree before they can move on and continue competing.

Many four year schools utilize junior college athletes to build their rosters with players that are ready to compete immediately. College teams prefer to recruit and develop high school players over 4 or 5 years, but sometimes circumstances dictate that they need to find players that are ready to step on campus and play immediately. For this, coaches will turn to junior colleges. Athletes that are looking for a fresh start, a chance to play, or the opportunity of continuing to develop, junior college football is the ideal route to go.

Most junior college teams will have a wide range of ability levels represented on their rosters. Typically, there will be a few DI caliber athletes who didn't qualify academically. They will have a few "drop-down" athletes from DI and DII programs that have come down to the JuCo level for a fresh start, second chance, because of poor grades or other problems. There will be future DII or DIII athletes that are trying to improve. There will be average athletes just out of high school that are looking to keep the dream alive or that also didn't qualify academically. There may be twenty-something year old men that are fresh out of the military, back from religious missions, or that are finally going to school. Junior college athletics will have a cornucopia of people and stories.

Coaching Changes

The reality of collegiate athletics is that coaches change jobs frequently. For most young coaches to move up the ladder, they have to change jobs. Coaches get fired for not performing. A football team has many, many coaches. Look on the practice field at a major football program and there will be the head coach, 8 assistants (coordinators & position coaches), graduate assistants, undergraduate assistants, quality control staff, interns, strength coaches, athletic trainers, volunteers, video staff, recruiting directors, equipment staff and even the operations director. Even lower level schools with minimal budgets have extensive coaching staffs. And when there are this many people involved, there will always be turnover. Top programs regularly have coaches recruited away by other schools.

If the head coach is fired, you can expect the majority of the coaching staff to also be released. Many of the lower level coaches, like graduate assistants and undergraduate volunteers, tend to be left alone, at least for a transitional period.

Athletes should NEVER go to a school just because of a coach. It can be one factor in the decision, but not the PRIMARY factor.

Depending on the timing of a coaching change, it can create a great deal of stress and anxiety for players. If a head coach leaves or is fired, this leaves the remaining staff in limbo. A period of uncertainty is normal and to be expected. It will be uncomfortable, but players should focus on being patient and calm. You can expect there to be lots of rumors. Teammates will voice their fears and make threats of transferring. Be calm. Let things play out. If it is around the Holidays, as this is when most coaching changes happen, go home and spend time with your family. Focus your time and energy worrying about things that you can control. You have no control over the decision of who will be the new coach.

With a head coaching change, you can expect there to be lots of new: new coaches, new offense and defense plays, new terminology, new techniques, new points of emphasis, new leadership style, and new slogans. The best thing you can do is to embrace the new. Players that fight change, end up getting pushed out. Don't be part of the problem, be part of the solution.

Recruiting Services
By Taylor Mitchell

If your child is being recruited by various schools to play in college athletics, there is also a strong chance that they are being recruited by different recruiting services or "agents" to help assist you with this process. I remember going through the recruiting process as a naive high school student-athlete and having no idea what direction to go or where to look for the various opportunities to play college football. Part of this process included talking to a recruiting service to see what they could do to help land me a scholarship. The answer our family quickly found was that this particular recruiting service would do everything I was already doing and would cost us several thousand dollars.

For some families, several thousand dollars for a service in exchange for tens of thousands of dollars in scholarship money is worth the risk. The risk/reward here makes it an extremely lucrative opportunity for families to pay these high fees for their "expertise." And this is what the recruiting services will promise you, the opportunity to play college athletics because of their connections and knowledge. The truth is that every kid that has landed an offer to play a college sport did so because of their athletic abilities. There are countless people that go into supporting these athletes contributing to them being able to receive an offer, but without being able to perform on the field, nothing else matters.

There are countless recruiting services available to student-athletes and families ranging from the National Collegiate Scouting Association (NCSA), Prep Stars, and Captain U. These services provide databases to college coaches and will flood their emails about various student-athletes. As a collegiate football coach, my Inbox is constantly filled with potential recruits that our staff should look at. Any high school student-athlete could have just as easily looked online for a coach's email and sent their highlights and information rather than paying for a service to do so.

After my first year as a college football coach, I found that I receive enough emails, phone calls, text messages and social media messages from recruits that I never had the time to use a recruiting service. A majority of the time when I received these generic emails, I found that these student-athletes were from all over the country and that most of them would not be a "fit" at our school or for our football program. These recruiting services compile a database of their customers or high school student-athletes and allow for college coaches to go through and search for potential recruits based on different information.

With college football continuing to grow in demand, recruiting departments and support staffs are also continuing to grow. The days of recruits "flying under the radar" or going "unnoticed" are over. The ease of access to information allows for coaches to hear about every top player in their key recruiting areas. Most top level college football programs use a variety of recruiting services where different scouts will pre-rank athletes so coaches can find what players may be a fit talent wise and evaluate these players.

For a majority of coaching staffs, their prospective student-

athletes have to meet certain criteria and benchmarks to be recruited to their school. These criteria and benchmarks can be made by the school, head coach or position coaches. A school may tell coaches that recruits need to meet certain GPA/test score standards, football coaches may only want players that meet certain measurable such as being 6' tall or the recruits have to play multiple sports. Some of these recruiting services allow for coaches to sift through thousands of kids to find the few that can play for their team. But, any email sent to a coach can include these key vitals that can make you stick out over other potential recruits.

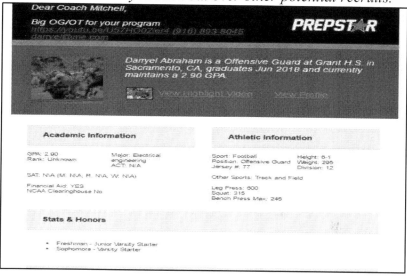

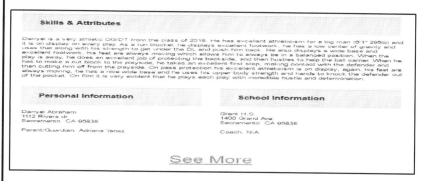

This was a common email that I would receive from the Prep Star recruiting service.

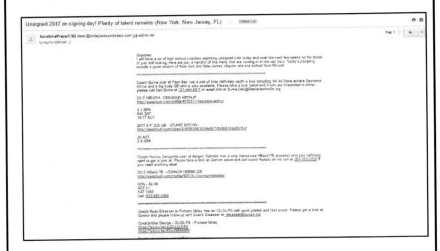

This email was from a "Recruiting Consultant" that parents and high school student-athletes were most likely paying to get them a scholarship. This Consultant was simply compiling a list of his clients and emailing them out to coaches. Is it worth the money?

Here is yet another example of a recruiting company "Sunshine Preps" sending a list of potential players left-over from signing day to every coach that they could find contact information on.

Conclusion

14

This book was born from our experience of a life lived with athletic children. At this time, two of our sons have finished their playing careers and two are still competing. They have each experienced some incredible highs and lows in their time, just as life will present to them after football is done. The oldest two had major reconstructive surgery to repair injuries from playing the game. Both will tell you that they did their absolute best with their God-given abilities and physique. They each have had to work extremely hard to get everything that they attained and are grateful to have played the game.

We never imagined any of this happening when they were toddlers. Nor could we envision all of the experiences that we and our sons would get to share. Traveling to visit college campuses, wondering where they each might wind up; getting that text or phone call about their first offer; making their commitment and signing their NLI; dropping them off at school; watching their first game; visiting new cities, campuses, and stadiums across the country; watching them play for the first time and for the last time. All of these are experiences that we are grateful to have shared with our children, because of football.

We have shared highs, lows, frustrations, disappointments, new experiences, new coaches, new schools, and new opportunities with our sons. Through it all, they have known our love for them was unwavering and unconditional. That it was based not on their performance, level of play, amount of playing time, or stats, but simply on the fact that they are our children. That we were proud of them for going for it, working hard, and pursuing their dreams. We've had the privilege of supporting and cheering for our children as they competed in a sport they love. And we plan to continue to cheer them on as they pursue all that life has to offer them.

Remember, playing the game of football will end for every player, but being part of a family will continue on. We pray that this book will keep you grounded and focused on the things that really matter: your family and your relationships. Enjoy the process of watching your son grow up, make choices, and work hard toward those. Love and support your children. Give them the space to both succeed and fail on their own. And always be there to guide and support them, whether in failure or success.

The following document, "My College Football Planner" should be used to help you develop your personal plan for pursuing college football opportunities.

My College Football Planner

Action List

- o   Talk to coach
- o   Meet with academic advisor
- o   Register with NCAA Clearinghouse (if needed)
- o   Study!
- o   Self-Assess
- o   FIT
- o   Highlight Film
- o   Network
- o   Communicate w/ Coaches
- o   Develop a Plan

Self-Assess

Physical attributes (DON'T LIE)

Height _____   Weight _____   40yd Dash _____
Strength _____

Athletic achievements:_____

_____

_____

_____

Varsity Letters? Awards?

_____

_____

_____

_____

Academics

GPA: _____ SAT _____ ACT: _____

Social Media & Pubic Image

Twitter, Facebook, Instagram, etc.

Google your name & high school

What do teachers, administrators & other coaches think of you?

FIT

What are YOUR Goals? Play, be part of team, "go for it", education, military academies

What position in college?

Type schools: Small, Private, Religious, Military, Specific Major

Level of play: D1, D2, D3, NAIA, Juco

Begin to research schools that FIT you, your goals, and your abilities

Develop School Wish List

A list (my reach list)

    1.

    2.

    3.

    4.

B list (my best fit)

    1.

    2.

    3.

    4.

C List (my fallback plan)

    1.

    2.

    3.

    4.

Highlight Film

Create a 3-5 minute highlight film that shows your athleticism, skill, hustle, best plays, and versatility

(Know that coaches watch how you FINISH plays, your effort)

NO need for music; trim plays down to the basics (no need to show 30 seconds of breaking the huddle and after a play), highlight yourself (if necessary)

Download final HUDL film for upload to YouTube (these display better for coaches)

Network

Who do I know that is playing college football or has played college football?

Choose athletes that have a similar position, level of projected play, or that are at schools that you are interested in attending.

Talk to parents of athletes who have been through the recruiting process.

Communicate with Schools & Coaches

First step is complete the questionnaire as a football prospect for each of my FIT schools

Identify who the recruiting coordinator is for each school.

Send email to coach along with highlight film link.

Look to visit schools during spring break, mid-winter break or during the summer. Arrange visits with coaches while checking out schools.

Come up with questions or conversation starters to help you when visiting campus or talking with a coach on the phone

- How do you recruit? When do you start? What are the things that you look for?
- How many players at my position to you look to bring in every year?
- Do you have a summer camp for prospects or recruits to visit and be evaluated?
- I'd like to visit campus sometime. When is a good time to visit and get to meet with coaches?

DEVELOP A PLAN

Craft a Self-Improvement Plan (things to work on)

Physical skills -

Strength -

Football skills -

Academics -

     GPA

     Core Classes

     ACT/SAT

Public Image -

Social Media Image -

Community service -

Create a College Exposure Plan

School Visits

Junior Days or Summer VIP Camps

College Visits & Game Day Visits

Regional Camps

Official visits or School overnight visits (D3)

List of College Football Programs
FBS Level (128 Teams)

Air Force	Florida	Minnesota	South Florida
Akron	Florida Atlantic	Ole Miss	USC
Alabama	Florida State	Mississippi State	SMU
Appalachian State	Georgia	Missouri	Southern Miss
Arizona	Georgia Southern	Navy	Stanford
Arizona State	Georgia State	Nebraska	Syracuse
Arkansas	Georgia Tech	Nevada	TCU
Arkansas State	Hawai'i	UNLV	Temple
Army West Point	Houston	New Mexico	Tennessee
Auburn	Idaho	New Mexico State	Texas
Ball State	Illinois	North Carolina	Texas A&M
Baylor	Indiana	NC State	Texas State
Boise State	Iowa	North Texas	Texas Tech
Boston College	Iowa State	NIU	UTEP
Bowling Green	Kansas	Northwestern	UTSA
Buffalo	Kansas State	Notre Dame	Toledo
BYU	Kent State	Ohio	Troy
California	Kentucky	Ohio State	Tulane
Fresno State	LSU	Oklahoma	Tulsa
UCLA	Louisiana Tech	Oklahoma State	Utah
UCF	Louisiana-Lafayette	Old Dominion	Utah State
Central Michigan	Louisiana-Monroe	Oregon	Vanderbilt
Charlotte	Louisville	Oregon State	Virginia
Cincinnati	Marshall	Penn State	Virginia Tech
Clemson	Maryland	Pittsburgh	Wake Forest
Colorado	Massachusetts	Purdue	Washington
Colorado State	Memphis	Rice	Washington State
Connecticut	Miami (FL)	Rutgers	West Virginia
Duke	Miami (OH)	San Diego State	Western Kentucky
Eastern Michigan	Michigan	San Jose State	Western Michigan
East Carolina	Michigan State	South Alabama	Wisconsin
FIU	Middle Tennessee	South Carolina	Wyoming

Lists of College Football Programs at FCS Level (125 Teams)

Abilene Christian	Florida A&M	Murray State	Stephen F. Austin
Alabama A&M	Fordham	New Hampshire	Stetson
Alabama State	Furman	Nicholls State	Stony Brook
Albany	Gardner-Webb	Norfolk State	Tennessee State
Alcorn State	Georgetown	North Carolina A&T	Tennessee Tech
Arkansas-Pine Bluff	Grambling State	North Carolina Central	Texas Southern
Austin Peay	Hampton	North Dakota	Towson
Bethune-Cookman	Harvard	North Dakota State	UC Davis
Brown	Holy Cross	Northern Arizona	UT Martin
Bryant	Houston Baptist	Northern Colorado	Valparaiso
Bucknell	Howard	Northern Iowa	Villanova
Butler	Idaho State	Northwestern State	VMI
Cal Poly	Illinois State	Penn	Wagner
Campbell	Incarnate Word	Portland State	Weber State
Central Arkansas	Indiana State	Prairie View A&M	Western Carolina
Central Connecticut	Jackson State	Presbyterian	Western Illinois
Charleston Southern	Jacksonville	Princeton	William & Mary
Chattanooga	Jacksonville State	Rhode Island	Wofford
The Citadel	James Madison	Richmond	Yale
Coastal Carolina	Kennesaw State	Robert Morris	Youngstown State
Colgate	Lafayette	Sacramento State	
Columbia	Lamar	Sacred Heart	
Cornell	Lehigh	Saint Francis	
Dartmouth	Liberty	Sam Houston State	
Davidson	Maine	Samford	
Dayton	Marist	San Diego	
Delaware	McNeese State	Savannah State	
Delaware State	Mercer	South Carolina State	
Drake	Mississippi Valley St.	South Dakota	
Duquesne	Missouri State	South Dakota State	
East Tennessee State	Monmouth	Southeast MO State	
Eastern Illinois	Montana	Southeastern Louisiana	
Eastern Kentucky	Montana State	Southern	
Eastern Washington	Morehead State	Southern Illinois	
Elon	Morgan State	Southern Utah	

Lists of College Football Programs at DII Level (170 Teams)

Adams State	Davenport	Lincoln
Albany State	Delta State	Lindenwood
Alderson Broaddus	Dixie State	Livingstone
American International	East Central	Lock Haven
Angelo State	East Stroudsburg	Long Island
Arkansas Tech	Eastern New Mexico	Malone
Arkansas at Monticello	Edinboro	Mars Hill
Ashland	Elizabeth City State	Mary
Assumption	Emporia State	McKendree
Augustana	Fairmont State	Mercyhurst
Azusa Pacific	Fayetteville State	Merrimack
Bemidji State	Ferris State	Michigan Tech.
Benedict	Findlay	Midwestern State
Bentley	Florida Institute of Tech.	Miles
Black Hills State	Fort Hays State	Millersville
Bloomsburg	Fort Lewis	Minnesota State Mankato
Bowie State	Fort Valley State	Minnesota State Moorhead
California	Gannon	Minnesota Crookston
Carson–Newman	Glenville State	Minnesota Duluth
Catawba	Grand Valley State	Minot State
Central Missouri	Harding	Mississippi
Central Oklahoma	Henderson State	Missouri Science and Tech.
Central State	Hillsdale	Missouri Southern State
Central Washington	Humboldt State	Missouri Western State
Chadron State	Indiana	Morehouse
Charleston	Indianapolis	Nebraska at Kearney
Cheyney	Johnson C. Smith	New Haven
Chowan	Kentucky State	New Mexico Highlands
Clarion	Kentucky Wesleyan	Newberry
Clark Atlanta	Kutztown	North Alabama
Colorado Mesa	Lake Erie	North Carolina at Pembroke
Colorado School of Mines	Lane	North Greenville
Colorado State Pueblo	Lenoir–Rhyne	Northeastern State
Concord	Limestone	Northern Michigan
Concordia–St. Paul	Lincoln	Northern State

List of College Football Programs at DII Level (170 Teams) Cont.

Northwest Missouri State	Texas A&M Commerce
Northwestern Oklahoma State	Texas A&M Kingsville
Northwood	Texas of the Permian Basin
Notre Dame	Tiffin
Ohio Dominican	Truman State
Oklahoma Baptist	Tusculum
Ouachita Baptist	Tuskegee
Pace	Upper Iowa
Pittsburg State	Urbana
Quincy	Valdosta State
Saginaw Valley State	Virginia State
Saint Anselm	Virginia Union
Saint Augustine's	Virginia's College at Wise
St. Cloud State	Walsh
Saint Joseph's	Washburn
Seton Hill	Wayne State
Shaw	Wayne State
Shepherd	West Alabama
Shippensburg	West Chester
Shorter	West Florida
Simon Fraser	West Georgia
Sioux Falls	West Liberty
Slippery Rock	West Texas A&M
SD School of Mines and Tech.	West Virginia State
Southeastern Oklahoma State	West Virginia Wesleyan
Southern Arkansas	Western New Mexico
Southern Connecticut State	Western Oregon
Southern Nazarene	Western State Colorado
Southwest Baptist	William Jewell
Southwest Minnesota State	Wingate
Southwestern Oklahoma State	Winona State
Stonehill	Winston–Salem State
Tarleton State	

Lists of College Football Programs at DIII Level (248 Teams)

Adrian	Carnegie Mellon	Ferrum	John Carroll
Albion	Carroll	Finlandia	Johns Hopkins
Albright	Carthage	Fitchburg State	Juniata
Alfred State	Case Western Reserve	Framingham State	Kalamazoo
Alfred	Castleton	Franklin and Marshall	Kean
Allegheny	Catholic	Franklin	Kenyon
Alma	Central	Frostburg State	King's
Amherst	Centre	Gallaudet	Knox
Anderson	Chapman	Geneva	La Verne
Anna Maria	Chicago	George Fox	LaGrange
Augsburg	Christopher Newport	Gettysburg	Lake Forest
Augustana	Claremont-Mudd-Scripps	Greensboro	Lakeland
Aurora	Coast Guard	Greenville	Lawrence
Austin	Coe	Grinnell	Lebanon Valley
Averett	Colby	Grove City	Lewis and Clark
Baldwin Wallace	Concordia (WI)	Guilford	Linfield
Bates	Concordia-Chicago	Gustavus Adolphus	Loras
Becker	Concordia-Moorhead	Hamilton	Louisiana College
Belhaven	Cornell	Hamline	Luther
Beloit	Cortland	Hampden-Sydney	Lycoming
Benedictine	Crown	Hanover	Macalester
Berry	Curry	Hardin-Simmons	MacMurray
Bethany	Defiance	Hartwick	Maine Maritime
Bethel	Delaware Valley	Heidelberg	Manchester
Birmingham-Southern	Denison	Hendrix	Maranatha Baptist
Bluffton	DePauw	Hiram	Marietta
Bowdoin	Dickinson	Hobart	Martin Luther
Bridgewater State	Dubuque	Hope	Mary Hardin-Baylor
Bridgewater	Earlham	Howard Payne	Maryville (TN)
Brockport	East Texas Baptist	Huntingdon	Mass-Dartmouth
Buena Vista	Elmhurst	Husson	Mass. Maritime
Buffalo State	Emory and Henry	Illinois College	McDaniel
Cal Lutheran	Endicott	Illinois Wesleyan	McMurry
Capital	Eureka	Iowa Wesleyan	Merchant Marine
Carleton	FDU-Florham	Ithaca	Methodist

Lists of College Football Programs at DIII Level (248 Teams) Cont.

Middlebury	Ripon	Utica
Millikin	Rochester	UW-Eau Claire
Millsaps	Rockford	UW-La Crosse
Minnesota-Morris	Rose-Hulman	UW-Oshkosh
Misericordia	Rowan	UW-Platteville
MIT	RPI	UW-River Falls
Monmouth	Salisbury	UW-Stevens Point
Montclair State	Salve Regina	UW-Stout
Moravian	Sewanee	UW-Whitewater
Morrisville State	Shenandoah	Wabash
Mount Ida	Simpson	Wartburg
Mount St. Joseph	Southern Virginia	Washington and Jefferson
Mount Union	Southwestern	Washington and Lee
Muhlenberg	Springfield	Washington U.
Muskingum	St. John Fisher	Waynesburg
N.C. Wesleyan	St. John's	Wesley
Nebraska Wesleyan	St. Lawrence	Wesleyan
Nichols	St. Norbert	Western Connecticut
North Central (Il)	St. Olaf	Western New England
North Park	St. Scholastica	Westfield State
Northwestern (MN)	St. Thomas	Westminster (Mo.)
Norwich	St. Vincent	Westminster (Pa.)
Oberlin	Stevenson	Wheaton (Ill.)
Occidental	Sul Ross State	Whittier
Ohio Northern	SUNY-Maritime	Whitworth
Ohio Wesleyan	Susquehanna	Widener
Olivet	TCNJ	Wilkes
Otterbein	Texas Lutheran	Willamette
Pacific Lutheran	Thiel	William Paterson
Pacific	Thomas More	Williams
Plymouth State	Trine	Wilmington
Pomona-Pitzer	Trinity (Conn.)	Wisconsin Lutheran
Puget Sound	Trinity (Texas)	Wittenberg
Randolph-Macon	Tufts	Wooster
Redlands	Union	Worcester State
Rhodes	Ursinus	WPI

Lists of College Football Programs at NAIA Level (86 Teams)

Arizona Christian Univ.	Faulkner University	University of Pikeville
Ave Maria University	Friends University	Point University
Avila University	Georgetown College	Presentation College
Bacone College	Graceland University	Reinhardt University
Baker University	Grand View University	Robert Morris University
Benedictine College	Hastings College	Rocky Mountain College
Bethany College	College of Idaho	St. Ambrose University
Bethel University	University of Jamestown	University of St. Francis (IL)
Bethel College	Kansas Wesleyan University	University of Saint Francis (IN)
Bluefield College	Kentucky Christian University	University of Saint Mary
Briar Cliff University	Langston University	Saint Xavier University
Campbellsville Univ.	Lindenwood University – Belleville	Siena Heights University
Carroll College	Lindsey Wilson College	Southeastern University
Central Methodist Univ.	Lyon College	Southern Oregon University
Cincinnati Christian Univ.	Marian University	Southwestern Assemblies of God
Concordia University (MI)	Mayville State University	Southwestern College
Concordia University (NE)	McPherson College	Sterling College
Culver–Stockton College	MidAmerica Nazarene University	Tabor College
Cumberland University	Midland University	Taylor University
Univ. of the Cumberlands	Missouri Baptist University	Texas College
Dakota State University	Missouri Valley College	Trinity International University
Dakota Wesleyan Univ.	Montana State University–Northern	Union College
Dickinson State University	Montana Tech of the UM	Valley City State University
Davenport University	University of Montana Western	Waldorf College
Doane College	Morningside College	Warner University
Dordt College	Northwestern College	Wayland Baptist University
Eastern Oregon University	Olivet Nazarene University	Webber International University
Edward Waters College	Ottawa University	William Penn University
Evangel University	Peru State College	

Lists of College Football Programs at NJCAA Level (66 Teams)

Arizona Western	Iowa Western CC
Arkansas Baptist	Itasca CC
ASA College	Itawamba CC
Blinn	Jones County JC
Butler CC	Kilgore
Central Lakes	Lackawanna
Cisco	Louisburg
Coahoma CC	Mesa CC
Coffeyville CC	Mesabi Range
DuPage	Minnesota State CTC
Copiah-Lincoln CC	Minnesota West CTC
Dakota College	Mississippi Delta CC
Dean	Mississippi Gulf Coast CC
Dodge City CC	Monroe
East Central CC	Nassau CC
East Mississippi CC	Navarro
Eastern Arizona	New Mexico Military Inst.
Ellsworth CC	North Dakota State College of Science
Erie CC	Northeast Mississippi CC
Fond du Lac	Northeastern Oklahoma A&M
Fort Scott CC	Northland CTC
Garden City CC	Northwest Mississippi CC
Georgia Military	Pearl River CC
Glendale CC	Phoenix
Globe Inst. of Tech.	Pima CC
Grand Rapids CC	Ridgewater
Highland CC	Rochester CTC
Hinds CC	Scottsdale CC
Holmes CC	Snow
Hudson Valley CC	Southwest Mississippi CC
Hutchinson CC	Trinity Valley CC
Independence CC	Tyler JC
Iowa Central CC	Vermilion CC

List of College Football Programs at CCCAA Level (69 Teams)

City College of San Francisco	El Camino College
College of San Mateo	Riverside City College
Santa Rosa Junior College	Citrus College
Diablo Valley College	Los Angeles Harbor College
Foothill College	Cerritos College
De Anza College	Allan Hancock College
Butte College	Bakersfield College
American River College	College of the Canyons
Feather River College	Moorpark College
College of the Siskiyous	Pasadena City College
Sacramento City College	Ventura College
Sierra College	Fullerton College
Fresno City College	Golden West College
Laney College	Grossmont College
Modesto Junior College	Palomar College
San Joaquin Delta College	Santa Ana College
College of the Sequoias	Orange Coast College
Chabot College	Saddleback College
Reedley College	Southwestern College
Hartnell College	Victor Valley College
West Hills College Coalinga	San Bernardino Valley College
Gavilan College	Mt. San Jacinto College
Monterey Peninsula College	San Diego Mesa College
Merced College	East Los Angeles College
Cabrillo College	College of the Desert
Los Medanos College	Compton College
Contra Costa College	Glendale Community College
Shasta College	Antelope Valley College
College of the Redwoods	Los Angeles Valley College
San Jose City College	Santa Barbara City College
Yuba College	Los Angeles Pierce College
Mendocino College	Santa Monica College
Long Beach City College	Los Angeles Southwest College
Mount San Antonio College	West Los Angeles College
Chaffey College	

Sources

Number of colleges and universities offering football reaches all-time high of 774 (2016, June 14). Retrieved from http://www.footballfoundation.org/tabid/567/Article/55626/Number-of-Colleges-and-Universities-Offering-Football-Reaches-All-Time-High-of-774.aspx